Identity and Community on
the Alaskan Frontier

LEE J. CUBA

Identity and Community on the Alaskan Frontier

TEMPLE UNIVERSITY PRESS

PHILADELPHIA

Temple University Press, Philadelphia 19122
Copyright © 1987 by Temple University. All rights reserved
Published 1987
Printed in the United States of America

The paper used in this publication meets the minimum requirements of
American National Standard for Information Sciences—Permanence
of Paper for Printed Library Materials, ANSI Z39.48-1984

Designed by Laury A. Egan

Library of Congress Cataloging-in-Publication Data

Cuba, Lee J.
    Identity and community on the Alaskan frontier.

    Bibliography: p.
    Includes index.
    1. Community organization—Alaska.   2. Group identity—Alaska.
3. Frontier and pioneer life—Alaska.   I. Title.
HN79.A58C83   1987   307.3'09798   86-14531
ISBN 0-87722-457-9 (alk. paper)

To Patty

ACKNOWLEDGMENTS

My research on Alaska began when I was a graduate student in the Department of Sociology at Yale University. There, I had the good fortune to study with three scholars whose sensitivity to the ways of community runs deep: Kai Erikson, Rosabeth Kanter, and Wendell Bell. A recent rereading of the manuscript by Erikson encourages me to believe that this book bears little resemblance to the doctoral thesis once submitted for their signatures, the plainest way I know to say that I continue to learn from their example.

Many others gave generously of themselves through an insightful reading of the entire manuscript, in particular John Hewitt, Albert Hunter, Jonathan Imber, Paul DiMaggio, Mark Miller, Susan Silbey, and Diane Vaughan. Their critical responses shaped the final form of the book, as did the helpful suggestions offered by Rosanna Hertz, Bernice Pescosolido, and Susan Watkins. Support for my initial fieldwork in Alaska was provided by a National Institute of Mental Health traineeship by Albert J. Reiss, Jr. Wellesley College funded a follow-up visit to Alaska, as well as a leave year during which I completed the manuscript.

My debt to Victor Fischer and Jane Angvik, who introduced me to Alaska, remains outstanding; their personal association with this work opened countless doors. The enthusiasm and support of other Alaskans, especially Michael Baring-Gould, Wendy Baring-Gould, Thomas Morehouse, Jack Peterson, and Suzan Nightingale, calmed the sometimes turbulent waters of fieldwork. To these, I add my sincere thanks to the scores of Anchorage residents from whose lives I constructed this story of Alaska. They forgot that I was an "Outsider" long enough to speak openly about their experiences, and, to my surprise, appeared as interested in my response to Alaska as I was in theirs.

At Temple University Press Jane Cullen held my hand through all of this and never tired of nor failed to answer my endless list of questions. Jennifer French, Nanette Bendyna, and others at the Press provided valuable editorial suggestions. Because I engaged her assistance to the point where I dared not ask for more, this is probably the only section of this book my wife, Patricia Ewick, will read. Through her substantial theoretical and editorial contributions, this book is as much hers as it is my own.

CONTENTS

INTRODUCTION

Although disciplinary boundaries are seldom well defined, few would hesitate to place the frontier within the domain of history. Perhaps this is a characterization peculiar to the United States, as it was an American historian—Frederick Jackson Turner—who drew attention to the frontier's importance in national development. Turner's work provoked a debate waged largely in the scholarly journals and professional meetings of historians. Some defended Turner's interpretation of the expansion of the American West, others challenged it, but the majority sought to modify it, accepting some issues as valid while recasting others. Most important, virtually no historian of nineteenth-century America *ignored* Turner's work, and it was this ubiquitous response that came to shape the study of frontiers in this century.

If the concept of "frontier" informed the vision of American historians, then its analogue among American sociologists must be the concept of "community." Like frontier, community was defined in ways sufficiently varied and numerous to allow for both broad application and repeated modification. The European intellectual tradition of the nineteenth century spawned an array of typologies that reflected changes in collective life associated with the passing of the Middle Ages: Maine's "status" and "contract," Marx's "feudal" and "capitalistic," Durkheim's "mechanical" and "organic," Weber's "traditional" and "legal-rational" forms of authority, and perhaps the most well remembered, Tönnies' "Gemeinschaft" and "Gesellschaft." Through variations of their own, American sociologists continued the conceptual tradition: Redfield's "folk-urban" continuum, Cooley's "primary group," and Parsons' "pattern variables of value orientation." In Europe these dichotomies provided the major analytic framework for charting the evolution of societies. In this country—where the sociological imagination was fixed on a particular moment in that evolution, that is, the growth and development of cities—they became synonymous with the study of society itself. Scholarly interest in the concepts of frontier and community centered on their loss, both as specific places and as representative of ways of life that they supported. The myth of the American frontier celebrates the virtues of rural, small-town life, and the ideological tradition shared by the concepts of frontier and community has informed our thinking about the quality of and prospects for modern society. At roughly the same time that American historians were proclaiming the passing of the landed frontier, American sociologists were documenting the demise of community. To their publics, these two groups intended both of these pronouncements as grim evidence of the irredeemable loss of a more meaningful way of life, and to their colleagues, these findings had the effect of reifying community, thereby diverting attention from the search for alternate forms of community in the modern world.

This book explores two paradoxes surrounding the debate over the loss of both frontier and community. The first concerns how historians have thought about frontiers, and the second concerns how sociologists have thought about community. Both groups have focused on how the currents of modern life have undermined rather than generated forms of frontier and community. In doing so, historians failed to appreciate the role urbanization played in defining the American frontier. Sociologists, by comparison, failed to acknowledge that new forms of community might arise in response to the dynamics of modern society. Using the example of contemporary Alaska, I will offer the counter-argument that the conditions of modern life help sustain the role of frontier and community in American society today. Because these two concepts are so closely related, reflecting on the meaning of the twentieth-century American frontier provides an opportunity to reassess the role of community in contemporary life: how it arises, what forms it assumes, and what significance it holds.

This line of reasoning suggests that we reconsider the role of place in discussions of community, especially in terms of its symbolic importance. By examining how cultural images can inhere in places (as is certainly true of "frontier" and Alaska), I hope to show that an important part of who we are is still derived from where we live. In Alaska and elsewhere, the symbolic aspects of place remain a viable source of both individual and collective identity.

The Contemporary Alaskan Frontier

From the time it was acquired by the United States in 1867, Alaska has been a likely candidate for an American frontier. And like the imagery surrounding the frontier itself, over a century later Alaska remains a place that defies simple description. Its half a million square miles embrace a diversity of climate, terrain, and population unparalleled by any other state: snow-capped mountains and hot springs; arid deserts and rain forests; 100-degree summer days and –60-degree winter nights; corporate officials peering out of glass skyscrapers and Natives clinging to a subsistence lifestyle. This immense variation is eclipsed only by the position of Alaska in the national imagination: vast regions of unexplored land harboring untapped energy reserves; a hope for new resources and new solutions to the problems of a troubled, aging society. No matter how fantastic the vision, Alaska seems large enough to encompass it.

This book describes one part of the Alaskan mosaic but, as I will maintain throughout, not an insignificant part of it. This Alaska belongs to a large yet relatively homogeneous group of state residents. The vast majority of them are white, and few are native to Alaska by birth. Even fewer are native in the cultural sense of that word—Indian, Aleut, or Eskimo. Most of them work in white-collar occupations, and as a group, they are among the best educated in the country. They live in suburban neighborhoods that resemble those found in most communities of the continental United States and depend on the same urban amenities that make such a life possible elsewhere. Is it anything more than mere fantasy, then, to claim that these Alaskan residents are America's contemporary pioneers?

The search for the exotic amid the everyday is very much alive in Anchorage, Alaska's largest city harboring roughly half of the state population. It has played a vital role in attracting migrants to Alaska, and it continues to weigh heavily in resident decisions to stay in the state. At the same time, the quest for a frontier experience proves a constant source of frustration for those residents of Anchorage who seek it. Even the most recent arrivals will have heard the familiar disparaging remarks of those living outside of Alaska's metropolitan center: "Anchorage is only an hour away from Alaska"; "I don't know any Alaskans living in Anchorage"; "Anchorage is our *American* city." Because their community so closely resembles other urban areas of the continental United States, Anchorage residents are sometimes called upon to demonstrate their uniqueness to others, as well as to themselves.

How they establish and sustain their claim as contemporary American pioneers provides the thesis for this book. The analysis that follows turns on the irony that the emergence of Alaska as a national frontier was possible only *after* Alaska had become urbanized. A tension between savagery and civilization spawned the American frontier ideal, and the relatively recent development of Anchorage as the economic and political center of Alaskan life did much to sharpen the contrast necessary to create the Alaskan frontier. At the same time, the taming of the Alaskan landscape represented in urban Anchorage engaged the processes of marginal differentiation essential to tying Alaska to the rest of the nation. Prior to that, Alaska proved too strange for most: more a foreign territory than an American frontier. Anchorage prospered because of this role of attaching Alaska to the continental United States; along with the revenues, resources, and people that passed between the two flowed the currency of cultural imagery.

It is this cultural image of the American frontier that makes Alaska provocative, because it illustrates how an *idea* can form the bases of community and identity. The values embodied in the American frontier ideal—resourcefulness, independence, openness, self-reliance, to name but a few—provide Anchorage residents with an image of what modern-day pioneers are like, defining the context for interaction with those living both in and outside of Alaska. In fact, one can safely say there are few aspects of life in Alaska that are not influenced by its image as a new American frontier. Its frontier image plays a major role in determining who will move to Alaska, as well as what they do once they arrive. It provides a lens through which they, and others, see themselves as contemporary pioneers. And it weighs heavily into their thoughts, decisions, and visions of Alaska's future. In short, it is impossible to overestimate the symbolic importance of the frontier to how Alaskans acquire a sense of self and to how they develop a sense of place.

The Organization of the Book

Because contemporary Alaskans are heirs to the frontier legacy, the book begins by tracing the history of this dominant cultural symbol. This intellectual tradition, which had its roots in Jeffersonian agrarianism and culminated in the frontier thesis of Turner at the end of the nineteenth century, developed alongside dramatic shifts in the national landscape. The ambiguity embedded in the metaphor of the frontier provided sufficient latitude to incorporate Alaska as a national frontier, a comfort for some who, like Turner, had declared the landed frontier closed at the end of the nineteenth century.

Whereas the first chapter explores the emergence of Alaska into the national system of cultural values, the second chapter focuses on its role as part of the national economic and political system. Alaska's strategic military location and natural resources served as the basis for increasing federal intervention, and the institutional developments that accompanied outside interest in Alaska established Anchorage as the undisputed center for economic activity in the region. The dominant role once occupied by the federal government in relation to Alaska as a whole has been assumed by Anchorage in relation to the remainder of the state.

The third and fourth chapters analyze the processes of group differentiation and identification that arise out of the structural factors linking Alaska to the rest of the country. Most of the people who live in Anchorage today have spent more time outside of Alaska than in it, and the move to Alaska consequently affords the opportunity to reflect on places left behind. In making this comparison, Anchorage residents often conclude that Alaska is unique among the fifty states and Alaskans singular among Americans. Chapter 3 (A Second Home: Anchorage as a Community of Migrants) describes the form this process of marginal differentiation takes and suggests that outsiders, as well as Alaskans, play an important role in maintaining the image of Alaska as an American frontier.

Chapter 4 (Becoming an Alaskan) extends the discussion of identity formation by describing how Anchorage residents mark differences among themselves. Newcomers to Anchorage pass through a series of reorientations of self involving language, space, and time on their way to achieving community membership. This process of residential identification cloaks Anchorage residents in the imagery surrounding the more primitive days of the Alaskan frontier and acts as a source of achieved status among long-time residents of the state.

Chapter 5 discusses the "selling" of the Alaskan image to other Americans. Because it occupies the status of a last American frontier in the minds of many, Alaska attracts migrants, visitors, and readers who long for a taste of the exotic. And as a result of its distant location from the rest of the nation, keeping that image alive (as well as converting it into monetary gains in the form of increased tourism and growing readerships) depends on the strategic control of information. In this way some Alaskans hope to moderate what they view as a historical pattern of exploitation of the frontier by those at the center of social life.

The book closes with an extended discussion of the paradoxes concerning "frontier" and "community" with which this Introduction began. Given the parallel traditions of these concepts, it is possible to read the twentieth century as a progressive search for community in a world that seems hostile to its presence. Americans have been reluctant to part with both the myth of the frontier and the nostalgia of small-town life, and this final chapter affords the opportunity to think beyond the case of Alaska to explore how these images provide a meaningful sense of community today.

The data analyzed in this book are drawn from a number of sources, both qualitative and quantitative, but they come principally from a random survey of Anchorage households conducted in 1979. For those interested in the details of the methods employed in this study, two research appendices are attached. The first appendix outlines the sampling procedures used to collect the Anchorage survey data and provides a descriptive profile of the residents interviewed. The interview schedule used in the Anchorage survey is reproduced in the second appendix.

Identity and Community on
the Alaskan Frontier

CHAPTER I

The Emergence of a National Idiom

The images surrounding the American frontier are as old as the settlements they describe, but the frontier as a national symbol failed to reach its dominant position in the cultural hierarchy until the frontier as fact had passed. The end of the nineteenth century brought with it the central dilemma confronting contemporary observers of the American landscape. As the cities on the eastern seaboard began to follow the course set by their European counterparts, as the rural West came more to resemble the urban East, and as a predominantly agrarian economy gave way to a primarily industrial one, the challenge to sustain a unique interpretation of American development accelerated. The history of the ascendance of the frontier as a cultural symbol is a history of comparatives, and in the face of what must have appeared a blurring of American and European, Western and Eastern, the search for a singular national idiom was all the more pressing.

In many respects reconciling the old with the new rekindled an ambivalence expressed in the tenets of Jeffersonian agrarianism, where the virtues of country life coexisted uneasily with the acknowledged importance of urban growth to the economic well-being of the nation. But the cities that Jefferson had in mind were unlike those emerging in the late nineteenth century, and correspondingly the debate over American symbols reached a stalemate. The current situation allowed no alternatives: the forces that would propel national life henceforth would reside in cities. A number of deeply rooted intellectual traditions came into play in response to what many viewed as the bleak historical realities of their time. The tensions that they represented—

between civilization and wilderness, urban and rural life, conformity and individualism—were never successfully resolved in the symbol of the American frontier. They are with us today, and they continue to frame our image of frontiers near the end of the twentieth century.

My purpose here is not to provide a detailed analysis of the historical and philosophical currents that had their fruition in the symbol of the American frontier.[1] It is necessary, however, to sketch the outlines of this tradition that culminated in the writings of Frederick Jackson Turner, the major proponent and most visible champion of the frontier myth, for Alaskans (if one can call them America's contemporary pioneers) are heirs to his legacy. The manner in which his image of the frontier was superimposed onto Alaska would, no doubt, have surprised Turner. At the end of the nineteenth century when Turner declared the western American frontier "closed," it was difficult to speak of Alaska as an American frontier in any meaningful sense; that time would not come for several decades. But in comparing the myths arising from the development of the continental United States and Alaska, one can find strong evidence of the tenacity with which Americans cling to their frontiers, even in times when the battles between civilization and savagery seem long since passed.

It is essential to bear in mind that much of what we know of frontiers has been seen through the eyes of those who made their homes in more established regions of the country. Their common task was to describe a place about which little was known, and consequently their accounts tell us something of how we see others who are strangers to us. Despite

1. For that, one may look to such substantial contributions as Henry Nash Smith's *Virgin Land: The American West as Symbol and Myth* (1950), Morton and Lucia White's *The Intellectual Versus the City: From Thomas Jefferson to Frank Lloyd Wright* (1977), Roderick Nash's *Wilderness and the American Mind* (1973), and Anselm Strauss's *Images of the American City* (1976). This brief summary of the intellectual history of "frontier" draws heavily on their work.

the insistence of one observer in 1834 that "the character and manners of the West . . . do not *essentially* differ from those of the population of the Atlantic States" (Baird, 1969), the majority were disposed to highlight the qualities that separated West from East. Because those who went looking for differences could be expected to find them, those who remained behind were left with the impression that life at the center of society must vary sharply from life at its edge.

The image of the frontier evolved out of the "paired but contradictory ideas of nature and civilization" (Smith, 1950:305). This juxtaposition of opposites was usually accompanied by a principle of forced choice; if one was to partake of life in either city or country, it would be had at a price. In the city, diverse and enriching experiences were coupled with a loss of personal independence; in the country, the renewal of spirit that accompanied daily confrontations with nature often proved tedious and dull.

This symbolic dichotomy, while conveying the essential elements of frontier imagery, is decidedly simplistic. Nature or wilderness (what Turner would refer to as "free land") acquired a number of representations over time: a source of fear and respect because of its primitive qualities, a harbinger of abundance and plenty because of its seemingly endless expanse, a haven of refuge that restored the soul. Likewise, the city, which was viewed as a hallmark of human progress, was denounced as variously too civilized and not civilized enough.[2] Changes in the imagery of nature versus civilization corresponded to historical shifts in the contours of national development, most notably advances in communications, transportation, and agricultural production. The predominant utility of these images lay in their supposed effects on individuals who inhabited both city and wild. This materialistic imperative was most forcefully argued by Turner, but the

2. The use of the word *denounced* is appropriate here because of the profound tradition of anti-urbanism in this country. See White and White (1977).

logical framework for it had been solidly established throughout the nineteenth century.

Although many observers of national development could be included in this history, I have focused on three: Thomas Jefferson, Ralph Waldo Emerson, and Henry David Thoreau. Each framed the duality of nature versus civilization in pivotal ways. Jefferson gives us a sense of the optimism that characterized late-eighteenth- and early-nineteenth-century views of the potentialities of the new nation. Emerson carried the discussion of the growth of American cities beyond the realm of economic necessity to the higher plane of intellectual discourse. And Thoreau celebrated the wildness of nature that those before him had viewed with disdain. In combination, their observations tell the story of how the promise associated with the largely rural pattern of western expansion shifted to a sense of alarm in the face of the growth and dominance of American cities in the latter half of the nineteenth century.

The Outlines of a Tradition

Thomas Jefferson's agrarian philosophy was not only a significant precursor to Turner's conclusions regarding the origins of pioneer democracy but also a reflection of the optimism that characterized late-eighteenth- and early-nineteenth-century views of the American West. At the turn of the century, the potentialities symbolized by the vacant lands of the West far outweighed their actual value. Secure in the belief that the frontier would not be populated for many centuries, Jefferson concluded that national development would not follow the same path as did European countries (Smith, 1950). Opening the land to small farmers meant that westward expansion would be dominated by a simple agricultural society, the pinnacle of the Jeffersonian ideal and the surest safeguard for democratic freedoms in the new republic. Echoing Crevecoeur's (1957) praise of

America as a land of "no aristocratic families, no courts, no
kings . . . no great manufactures employing thousands," Jefferson continued the tradition of making sharp distinctions
between America and the continent. Similar descriptions
would be eloquently stated by Tocqueville (1956:53) two
decades later:

> In the Western settlements we may behold democracy
> arrived at its utmost limits. In the States, founded
> off-hand, and as it were by chance, the inhabitants are
> but of yesterday. Scarcely known to one another, the
> nearest neighbors are ignorant of each other's history.
> In this part of the American continent, therefore, the
> population has escaped the influence not only of great
> names and great wealth, but even of the natural aris-
> tocracy of knowledge and virtue. None are there able to
> wield that respectable power which men willingly grant
> to the remembrance of a life spent in doing good before
> their eyes. The new States of the West are already
> inhabited; but society has no existence among them.

If Jefferson's concern for the well-being of the nation
fueled his passion for yeoman husbandry, it also opened his
eyes to the necessity of urban, industrial development to
economic self-sufficiency. "For the general operations of
manufacture, let our workshops remain in Europe," he wrote
near the end of the eighteenth century. But the War of 1812
made it clear that dependence on the "workshops of Europe"
perpetuated colonial status of the new nation. By 1816 he
concluded, "We must now place the manufacturer by the side
of the agriculturist." Yet to experience the dynamic forces of
industrial production, Jefferson envisioned a nation sufficiently vast to allow for population growth different from
that of Europe:

> It does not follow, that with a territory so boundless, it
> is the interest of the whole to become a mere city of
> London. . . . The agricultural capacities of our country

constitute its distinguishing feature; and the adapting of our policy and pursuits to that, is more likely to make us a numerous and happy people, than the mimicry of an Amsterdam, a Hamburgh, or a city of London. (quoted in White and White, 1977:18–19)

When Jefferson penned his first remarks about the evils of cities, the population of the United States was something under 4 million. Only six cities harbored 8,000 or more inhabitants, and about three out of every 100 Americans resided in cities. By 1840 the census recorded a national population of over 17 million, a figure that would more than double by 1870. Whereas the percentage of persons living in urban areas remained relatively small (approximately 9 percent), the number of urban centers had increased almost eight-fold to forty-four (Weber, 1967:20). The fears that haunted Jefferson had become the realities of Ralph Waldo Emerson and Henry David Thoreau. The centuries of rural comfort predicted by Jefferson had proved to be little more than wishful prophecy.

Like Jefferson, Emerson lived with an unresolved ambivalence concerning the role of cities in the rapidly expanding nation. But unlike his predecessor, Emerson's perspective of city life was influenced by the tenets of a metaphysical philosophy rather than by the practical need for urban manufacturing. His reservations are most clearly expressed in the distinction he makes between two kinds of knowledge: Understanding and Reason. *Understanding* "toils all the time, compares, contrives, adds, argues; near-sighted but strong-sighted, dwelling in the present, the expedient, the customary." By contrast, *Reason* "never reasons, never proves; it simply perceives; it is vision" (quoted in White and White, 1977:25). Reason informs the higher orders of philosophy and poetry, and Understanding guides the mechanical thought of the technician. Reason resides in the country, Understanding in the city:

The city delights the Understanding. It is made up of finites: short, sharp, mathematical lines, all calculable.

It is full of varieties, of successions, of contrivances. The Country, on the contrary, offers an unbroken horizon, the monotony of an endless road, of vast uniform plains, of distant mountains, the melancholy of uniform and infinite vegetation; the objects on the road are few and worthless, the eye is invited ever to the horizon and the clouds. It is the school of Reason. (quoted in White and White, 1977:25)

The contrast between city and country embodied in this philosophical dualism furthered the devaluation of urban life in the face of rural enterprise. The ties to the land represented in agricultural production were extended to encompass the rebirth of character associated with even limited contact with the countryside, and the tentative acceptance of urban commerce and manufacture gave way to a broader attack on the artificiality of city life in general. As with Jefferson, Emerson viewed the core of the American character as residing in "the kind of man the country turns out" (quoted in White and White, 1977:26). Valued traits of honesty, virtue, and self-determination stemmed from contact with the rural.

Emerson, nonetheless, could not dispense with the utility of cities entirely. Though inherently artificial, cities also afforded some measure of scholarly vitality—schools, museums, lectures. "I wish to have rural strength and religion for my children, and I wish city facility and polish. I find with chagrin that I cannot have both" (quoted in White and White, 1977:27). Emerson never resolved this dilemma, but he believed that others, like his friend Henry David Thoreau, had managed to free themselves from the corrupting influence of city life.

Neither Jefferson nor Emerson (nor scores of other visitors to the borders of nineteenth-century America) mentioned the virtues of untamed wilderness in their praise of country life. In fact, the rural virtues they extolled were a direct consequence of the taming of a hostile wilderness. Thoreau, by contrast, envisioned a good life in which the country occupied a middle ground between savagery and civilization.

"Wildness and refinement were not fatal extremes but equally beneficent influences Americans would do well to blend" (Nash, 1973:95). In straddling the gap between city and wild, Thoreau celebrated both the wilderness and the place of the frontier in defining the wild.

The growing commercialism of the mid-1800s drove Thoreau from the cities in search of a revitalization of spirit. Life in the wild was free of encumbrances; it forced a self-reliance conducive to the complete realization of human potential. "Our lives . . . need the relief of [the wilderness] where the pine flourishes and the jay still screams" (quoted in Nash, 1973:87). Thoreau encouraged his contemporaries to seek out landed frontiers, as well as to create their own frontiers of a higher order. If a frontier was "wherever a man *fronts* a fact," the wilderness nevertheless provided the solitude essential to that search for inner strength. It was the proper environment, as Thoreau put it, for living "deliberately."

Thoreau's enthusiasm for this "frontier experience" extended to his expectations for the nation as a whole (Nash, 1973). The tameness of the continent had resulted in the stagnation of the European spirit; immigrants to America, by contrast, faced a continent of limitless potential. All that was required to benefit from this unique opportunity was a conscientious attempt to pursue life seriously and purposively.

This hopeful enthusiasm concerning the revitalizing role of the American frontier extended far beyond the narrow circles of intellectual discourse. In the latter half of the nineteenth century, the frontier became a widely used metaphor for American progress and success. It was incorporated into the speeches of local and national politicians, used to defend the preservation of wilderness areas, heralded as the foundation of small-town life, and eventually associated with the development of urban centers throughout the country. As population shifted westward, the setting associated with the frontier assumed various forms as well—from agricultural settlements to railroad centers to mining camps.

These changes in the focus of the image of the frontier corresponded to changes in the landscape of the nation. In 1850 the United States contained eighty-five cities with a population of 8,000 or more, representing roughly 12.5 percent of the country's total population. By 1890 the number of urban areas had increased to 448, together containing over 29 percent of the national population (Weber, 1967). Various westward migrations occurred during this forty-year period as a response to expanded agricultural and mining activities, but the population development from 1880 to 1890 was largely industrial, with migration primarily directed toward urban areas. Farm production became a commercial, non-subsistence occupation as crop specialization increased and advances in transportation weakened the need for agricultural self-sufficiency (Strauss, 1976). Cities, particularly those in the East, came to resemble more closely their European counterparts as manufacturing became the driving force of the national economy. And as midwestern towns developed into marketplaces for the exchange of local goods and services rather than serving as mere distribution centers for outlying regions, they assumed a function and form not unlike those of older established cities on the eastern seaboard.

No wonder, then, that as the geographic frontier was quickly disappearing from the American landscape, some would fight to resurrect it as a national symbol and even use it to describe cities that had for so long been portrayed as the antithesis of the frontier.

A Synthesis: Turner's Frontier Thesis

It was out of this heritage that historians of the twentieth century were to compare the frontiers of Europe and America. This comparison was the focus of Frederick Jackson Turner's frontier thesis, which became the topic of much controversy, both popular and scholarly, soon after he delivered his memorable address in 1893. One of the primary reasons his thesis was so vigorously debated had to do with its appeal to the public in general, for as one historian has noted, "Turner captured the historic images that others had lost sight of" (Welter, 1961:6). Turner was saying something that Americans were eager to hear, that the differences between themselves and Europeans were inherently tied to the colonization of the United States. The hardships that confronted the American settlers were, at least in part, the demands required to tame a hostile wilderness.[3]

America was unique, Turner maintained, because it contained a large area of free land that was constantly receding in the wake of national settlement. With each advance of the population, society was forced to begin again as men and women attempted to recreate familiar forms of social organization in unfamiliar settings. Because the American pioneers were more concerned with establishing the rudiments of community than with pursuing the cultural niceties of a more refined society, economic and political controls were kept to a minimum. Thus, communities in the East had a different structure from those in Europe, and those in the West were correspondingly different from those in the East. As the population increased, community differences became less noticeable, but that was not to say that the frontier experience had not left its mark on western settlements. This "Americanization" of the people and their institutions would persist long after the availability of free land had disappeared. (According to Turner, the country had reached that point by the end of the nineteenth century.)

3. This is not to suggest that Turner was arguing a case for mono-causation. There is evidence in his essays that Turner considered the settlement of the American West one of several factors that shaped the national character. He does, however, devote the majority of his analysis to a study of westward expansion.

Although others had made similar observations concerning the importance of wilderness conditions to the distinctive character of Americans, Turner was the first to state these effects in an explicitly causal manner. Put simply, he argued that the environment effected certain changes in the settlers, who in turn shaped their social, political, and economic institutions in a peculiar American fashion. This process was accomplished in a variety of ways. Old ways of doing things were discarded when appropriate, and new, more practical solutions were substituted. When traditional methods were retained, they continued in modified forms that were adapted to the special circumstances of frontier life.

Much of the debate over Turner's work stemmed from his loose usage of "frontier," a concept defined in various ways in his many essays. The frontier appeared as "the meeting ground between savagery and civilization," "the temporary boundary of an expanding society at the edge of substantially free lands," "a migrating region," a "form of society," a "state of mind," a "stage of society rather than a place," a "process," "the region whose social conditions result from the application of older institutions and ideas to the transforming influences of free land," and "the margin of settlement which has a density of two or more to the square mile" (Billington, 1958). By ignoring the historical meaning of the concept and substituting a flexible definition for one more precise, Turner was able to further emphasize the distinctions between Europe and America that he considered essential in his statement of the frontier thesis.

Types of Frontiers

Turner's analysis is confusing because in describing the frontier in numerous and different ways, he was referring to three distinct types of frontiers. The first denoted a *geographic territory* with identifiable physical characteristics (e.g., "a migrating region," "the margin of settlement which has a density of two or more to the square mile"); the second, a peculiar *set of social conditions* resulting from human interaction with the environment (e.g., "a form of society," "a stage of society rather than a place"); and the third, a *subjective response to place* as manifested in individual attitudes and beliefs (e.g., "a state of mind").

Because he failed to distinguish analytically among these three types of frontiers, Turner did not envision the possibility that a place marked by the physical characteristics of a frontier may be populated by those who do not think of themselves as "frontiersmen." That is, they fail to interpret the experiences of everyday life in terms of a frontier ideology. Logically, the opposite situation is also possible: persons may adopt a frontier "state of mind" apart from a daily routine that necessitates coping with primitive living conditions.

I will suggest shortly that this latter case more accurately describes life in contemporary Alaska. But first, it is essential to note the origin of the types of frontiers outlined, their applicability to the frontier thesis, and their subsequent use by social theorists to describe patterns of pioneer settlement.

Frontier as Territory

The initial English usage of *frontier*—probably dating back to about 1400—lacked any evaluative connotations. Instead, it simply described the military or political limits of a region. Over time, the frontier was more generally defined as a border region at the edges of a civilization or a boundary line between nations (Juricek, 1960). Frontier as "border" usually referred to a territory belonging to a single country or people, whereas frontier as "boundary" described a geographic line shared by several countries. The "border" connotations of the early definition were clearly ethnocentric in the sense that they set the limits of a people's known world. With the development of nation-states in the seventeenth century, however, the subsequent "boundary" definition of frontier increased in popular usage because of its utility in describing the relationship *between* peoples. Order emerged out of chaos, and previously vague borderlands between nations merged into distinct frontier lines or "common frontiers" (Clark, 1947). The military connotations of frontier were replaced by political ones. Disputes were resolved through the continual charting of maps, with diplomacy requiring an international rather than a national vocabulary.

Given this linguistic tradition, the early settlers came to America with a clear notion of what a frontier was. Although the original colonies were established on the eastern coast of a vast continent, the frontier of colonial America did not extend for miles to the west. Instead, it was bounded by a series of Indian nation frontiers and thus bordered not by emptiness but rather by other recognized countries (Juricek, 1960). When eighteenth- and nineteenth-century observers recounted sagas of frontier life in America, their concern was with life at the edges of an established settlement.

It was Turner who first attributed a peculiar set of physical characteristics to the American frontier. His writings give us the impression that the wilderness that greeted the pioneers was a hostile one, that the areas they charted were largely unsettled, and that the frontier regions abounded with natural resources of all kinds—forests, mountains, arable land, minerals, and wildlife (Pierson, 1940). Although scholars have since challenged the historical accuracy of Turner's description of frontier life, most of their criticisms have addressed his analysis of social institutions and their effects on the development of the American character. Consequently, the image of the frontier as a dangerous and potentially exploitable region has remained the dominant cultural view of the American West.

Frontier as Form of Society

The second way in which Turner used *frontier* derived its importance from the social-organizational correlates of the physical conditions faced by the pioneers, rather than from the actual characteristics of the place itself. His analysis of the frontier circumstances facing the settlers focused primarily on the deterministic qualities of the environment, viewing the development of a unique American character as the result of individual adaptations to a new environment.[4] Thus, the pioneer's response to a rough land required inventive solutions, hard work, and physical and psychological endurance. The presence of a sparse frontier population necessitated self-reliance and individualism. These individual accommodations were, in turn, manifested in collective form: the relative absence of cultural institutions (e.g., art, science, literature); the partial disintegration of economic and legal institutions (revised attitudes toward lending corporations and agents of social control); and the birth of new forms of political association (national interest and the rise of "frontier democracy") (cf. Pierson, 1942). One is left with the impression that the pioneers were loners who abandoned an old world in search of a new one, with a deep self-centeredness their most valuable asset in the struggle with a fierce environment.

Of course, many critics have questioned the validity of Turner's generalizations regarding frontier life. There is good reason to believe that communalism was more important

4. This issue is similar to one that concerned Park and other American sociologists of the Chicago School near the beginning of the century. They observed that physical space is often correlated with social (and even psychological) space and that, as a result, physical distance provided a rough measure of social distance. Because the frontier is always geographically distant from the center of a nation, the inhabitants of these marginal regions were thought to act and think differently from those who compose the majority of society. This is essentially a deterministic approach, making the case that the environment exerts a powerful influence on thought and action.

than individualism in the shaping of nineteenth-century American settlements (Boatright, 1941), that "frontier democracy" was considerably less democratic given the importance of leadership and social networks in the events governing small-town life (Leyburn, 1935; Loomis, 1940; cf. Elkins and McKitrick, 1954), and that "free land" did not serve to liberate vast numbers of urban-industrial laborers (Shannon, 1945; Kane, 1936; cf. Schafer, 1937; Smiler, 1958). In short, most challenges to the frontier thesis concerned Turner's overemphasis of the *discontinuities* between life in the established regions of America and pioneer society. The familiar ways of community were no less important in the West than in the East, and the continuity that persisted between the old and the new figured prominently into the lives of the settlers:

> Institutional changes might have been greater if the men who led the West had sought a new country more than they sought individual self-realization and self-improvement. In general they were neither refugees nor entirely exiles. New York or Pennsylvania was still a second home. Coming in hope rather than fear or bitterness, often with some small stake for the new venture, members of a fairly homogeneous culture, they had little in common with Indians moved from their hereditary lands, or with convicts transported from Europe. Seeing the vigor of individual aspiration, historians sometimes have assumed too readily that Westerners wished to cut themselves off from eastern ways. (Pomeroy, 1966:82–83)

All of this is not to say that frontier settlements were mere reproductions of eastern communities, for the very real wilderness conditions of the frontier required a certain amount of courage, determination, and practical inventiveness on the part of newcomers. Some have argued, however, that any or all of the pioneers' accommodations to new surroundings are attributable to the process of migration and are not the consequence of a unique "westering experience" (Lee, 1961;

Pierson, 1973). Starting over—and all that it entails—is not solely endemic to frontier migration but is a general quality of migration to any destination. These critics maintain that any consequences arising out of a move westward might best be viewed as a result of a general process rather than attributable to the effects of a specific place.

Regardless of which perspective one adopts, the basic task of both historian and sociologist remains the same when considering the frontier as a form of society—that of seeking a relationship between social or physical structure and forms of individual and collective association.

Frontier as State of Mind

In his work on frontier territories, Turner had little to say about the subjective qualities of the frontier experience. This is perhaps attributable to the deterministic bias evident in his frontier thesis, where his principal concern was with the contextual effects of the American West on the pioneers. Frontier as "state of mind" implies the opposite of this; it is instead a perspective that suggests that individuals create, shape, and distort their surroundings through their perceptions of the world. Culture is not determined by ecology, biology, social structure, or any combination of these. It is a product of the interaction of these with personal or collective expectations of and responses to a place. As such, "frontier" has come to symbolize a way of life that forms an established part of American culture.

Scholars of various disciplines have recognized this phenomenon. Geographers have referred to it as "image geography," the process by which the terrain and climate of a region come to live in the dreams of its people. The land becomes what we see in it, what we want from it, and what we make of it (Watson, 1970). Psychologists have noted similar patterns in their analyses of "subjective culture," the subjective responses (myths, roles, values, and attitudes) to what is man made (Triandis, 1972). And sociologists have dealt with the manner in which we interpret the realities of everyday life in their queries concerning a "sociology of knowledge" (Berger and Luckmann, 1967). As applied to the frontier case, the focus shifts from characteristics of landscape, population density, and institutional development to personal traits of independence and self-reliance often associated with residents of frontier territories.

The primary illustration of frontier conceived of in this sense is found in Evon Vogt's (1955) analysis of a New Mexico community established in the early 1930s. Vogt used a Parsonian model to describe the value orientations held in common by the settlers. As witnessed in the behavior of the community members, he noted "a strong stress upon *individualism;* an accent upon *hopeful mastery over nature;* a patterned balance between *working and loafing;* an emphasis upon the *future;* and a combination of *group-superiority and group-inferiority* in their relation with other cultural groups" (Bogue, 1968:81). In Vogt's estimation, adherence to these value orientations was leading to the disintegration of the community. The validity of this interpretation has been challenged on the grounds that Vogt overemphasized the salience of values and their impact on the behavior of the homesteaders (Bogue, 1968), but the point remains that the settlers' response to the frontier experience was affected by their view of their location in physical and social space.

Conceptualizing the frontier as a subjective phenomenon distinguishes Turner the historian–social scientist from Turner the mythmaker, a scholar remembered not only for his causal analysis of the effects of a frontier environment but also for his success in extolling and popularizing the vision of the pioneer as paragon of all American virtues (Benson, 1969). By asserting that America had witnessed the passing of the frontier by the end of the nineteenth century, Turner failed to acknowledge the firmness with which the *image* of the frontier had been grounded in American culture. In doing so, he underestimated the strength with which ideologies persist. At the same time, he could not have anticipated the extent to which his work would influence this image of frontier. As one student of the controversy surrounding the frontier thesis noted:

> The . . . debate over what Turner actually meant and over the truth or falsity of his hypothesis is much more than a mere academic quibble. It concerns the image of themselves which many—perhaps most—Americans of the present day cherish, an image that defines what Americans think of their past, and therefore what they propose to make of themselves in the future. (Smith, 1950:4)

Turner and the Alaskan Frontier

Turner devoted his professional life to cataloguing the peculiar characteristics of the American frontier, but his enduring legacy was to expand the meaning of frontier to such an extent that almost no place would fail to qualify as a rough boundary marking the edge of national progress. And although he may have predicted that Alaska would come to occupy such a role in this century, he clearly did not identify it as an important American frontier in his own writing. His work focuses exclusively on the significance of westward expansion across the continental United States. *The Frontier in American History* (1920) includes only a single reference to Alaska, a prophetic aside appearing in a reprint of his commencement address delivered at the University of Washington in 1914: "Already Alaska beckons on the north, and pointing to her wealth of natural resources asks the nation on what new terms the new age will deal with her" (1920:296).

If Alaska did little more than "beckon on the north" near the beginning of this century, it assumed this minor role in the American frontier story because of both the peculiar quality and scant quantity of information available to Turner and others searching for new frontiers. Like the many reports of California gold rush experiences that drifted back to the eastern seaboard, the tales of early Alaska were infused with the local color of the mining camp. But unlike the analogous literary tradition of the American West, the literature of Alaska focused on the region's untamable wildness. Most of Alaska was not, to use Turner's phrase, "capable of conquest." Survival on the Alaskan frontier meant learning to adapt to wilderness conditions; it did not entail subduing the wild (Jody, 1969).

This was the repeated message carried back by visitors to Alaska, whether it echoed the rough-hewn grit of Jack London or the new breed of transcendentalism characteristic of John Muir. The agrarian tradition that gave birth to the myths surrounding westward expansion had no place in the saga of Alaskan development. Instead, the harsh and vast terrain of Alaska prohibited large-scale agricultural production. Caricatures of Alaska were engulfed in a "literary fog" that perpetuated the romanticism associated with resource exploration in the region (Byrns, 1961).

This fascination with the wildness of Alaska continues today. Because the pattern of migration that closed the West as a frontier in the nineteenth century cannot be replicated in Alaska, it is a perfect repository for the American frontier image. Alaska stands as a lasting set of challenges, ranging from massive institutional efforts to tap the wealth of its natural resources to the singular personal quest for a new life. Those who respond to these challenges are likely to begin their search in Anchorage, Alaska's largest city.

CHAPTER 2

Anchorage, Alaska

Anchorage is sometimes excused in the name of pioneering. Build now, civilize later. But Anchorage is not a frontier town. It is virtually unrelated to its environment. It has come in on the wind, an American spore. A large cookie cutter brought down on El Paso could lift something like Anchorage into the air. Anchorage is the northern rim of Trenton, the ocean-blind precinct of Daytona Beach. It is condensed, instant Albuquerque. (McPhee, 1977)

In contrast with the American West of the nineteenth century, the history of the Alaskan frontier is not one of pioneers who subdued a hostile wilderness. Alaska was never the site of a constantly shifting frontier zone where life began anew with each great migration of newcomers. It never harbored large regions of arable land that, when cultivated, would stand as a visible sign of national progress. Instead, the settlement of Alaska has resembled less the mastering of a territory and more the establishment of footholds in a largely uninhabitable region. Since the beginning of this century, each surge of population into the area has receded into one of three regional centers—Juneau in southeastern Alaska, Fairbanks in the interior, or Anchorage in south central Alaska.

One is tempted to attribute the peculiar nature of Alaska's development to environmental factors, and to some extent such an assertion is justified. The landscape of Alaska is one of immense climatological and topographical variation; the exploration for and discovery of Alaskan resources sparked a search for appropriate solutions to the housing, transportation, and agricultural needs of early settlers. The first towns of substantial size grew up around sites of resource development. Kodiak and Sitka, both centers of commerce for Russian America in southeast Alaska, were established to facilitate fur trading with Native Alaskans. After the United States purchased Alaska in 1867, Juneau and Nome served as headquarters for the first mining operations in the territory. The discovery of gold farther inland led to the settlement of Fairbanks in 1903.

Unlike with these other major communities, the birth and subsequent development of Anchorage were not directly related to the diverse natural resources that formed the basis for outside interest in Alaska. Anchorage was born out of a decision made by the federal government to link interior Alaska to the coast by means of a railroad. Those who travelled to Ship's Creek[1] in the spring of 1915 came not in search of gold or furs but in search of construction work. What provided the initial impetus for this small town in south central Alaska—the need to service other, more remote areas of the region—was to become its identifying mark in future years. Despite periods of boom and bust, interest and disinterest, Anchorage prospered because of its central role in attaching Alaska to the rest of the nation. As the level of technology progressed, the means of attachment shifted—from rail and marine transportation to aviation. The source of institutional support also reflected these changes, as the role played by railroad construction in the first twenty-five years of community life gave way to the influence of the military in the next twenty-five years.

The rise and dominance of Anchorage as the center of economic and political activity in Alaska illustrate dramatically that outside interest, and not environmental factors, has been the driving force in Alaska's development. The primary mover in this historical progression has been the federal government. Under territorial status it controlled approximately 99 percent of Alaskan lands; after statehood, it retained ownership of over 60 percent of Alaska. This overwhelming reliance on outside interest, while fostering the

1. Ship's Creek was the early name for Anchorage.

dependence of Alaska on federal intervention, secured a dominant position for Anchorage in local affairs. Just as Anchorage became the major recipient of federal assistance (and, for that reason, perhaps the principal symbol of a dependence that characterized the region as a whole), the remainder of Alaska assumed a position of *internal* dependence on Anchorage. Because it stands at the intersection of Alaskan development and federal control, Anchorage occupies a pivotal role in the history of American involvement in Alaska.

The urbanization of Anchorage represents one of the central ironies of Alaskan life, for without it, one could reasonably assert that Alaska would never have received national attention. The many improvements in transportation, housing, and communication that accompanied outside investment in Alaska from World War II to the present drew Alaska into the web of national affairs. And while these changes led to the characterization of Anchorage as a "non-Alaskan" city, they simultaneously "Americanized" Alaska to make it a viable actor—both politically and economically—in national life. This attachment to the continental United States was a necessary first step in identifying Alaska as an American frontier.

Growth and Development in South Central Alaska

The historical sketch that follows documents the progression of events that transformed a tent town of less than 2,000 into a city housing nearly half of Alaska's population. It is devoid of the undoubtedly more colorful side of Alaska's past: tales of Native cultures; sagas of Russian exploration; legends of boomtown miners, loggers, and trappers.[2] Instead, it is a history of institutional development in Alaska over the past seventy years.

2. In fact, it is difficult to find historical accounts of Anchorage in its early years because few histories of Alaska mention Anchorage specifically.

Although these events are presented in chronological order, they were not of equal consequence to the development of Anchorage. Instead, they represent three distinct types of growth in south central Alaska. First, railroad and defense construction in south central Alaska are the principal events in this history, as they established Anchorage as the primary transportation center in the territory. Not only was railroad construction responsible for the birth of Anchorage, but it also spawned the first major community in Alaska not established directly at the site of a resource production area. Military construction in the 1940s and 1950s secured Anchorage's position as the center for air transport in Alaska and, in signalling the shift from resource production to government-related activity, proved to be the single most important boom toward the urbanization of the region.

Second, and of lesser significance, were the experimental farming colony established in the Matanuska Valley in 1935 and the federal disaster relief program following the Good Friday earthquake of 1964. Neither of these measures of government assistance left deep impressions on the landscape of south central Alaska. Instead, they carried the Anchorage economy through dormant periods. In this respect they typified the continuing dependence of Alaska on the federal government.

Finally, the discovery of oil in northern Alaska—the event most often associated with the state today—clearly illustrates the benefits accruing to Anchorage from resource develop-

A sample of thirteen histories of Alaska written in the first half of this century revealed only two that mentioned Anchorage (or Ship's Creek). Consequently, most of the information in this chapter is taken from more recent sources. The following were particularly helpful: Anchorage Resource Information Service (1978), Atwood (1957), Alaska Criminal Justice Planning Agency, State of Alaska (1979), Gardey (1976), Gruening (1954), Hanrahan and Gruenstein (1977), Kresge, Morehouse, and Rogers (1977), Hunt (1976), Rogers (1970). Numerous articles from the *Anchorage Times* and the *Anchorage Daily News* were also useful.

ment elsewhere in Alaska. By the late 1960s, Anchorage was firmly established as the leading commercial center in the state, making it the logical choice for the corporate head-quarters of oil and gas companies. Whereas Fairbanks (the center for pipeline construction in Alaska) experienced a sharp decline in both population and service industries after completion of the pipeline, Anchorage, after a brief economic downturn, continued to prosper. The pipeline experience assured Alaskans that future development in their state would be measured by the impact it registered in Anchorage.

The Alaska Railroad

Alaskans had been complaining for some time about a lack of internal transportation routes when Congress authorized the building of the Alaska Railroad in 1912. Just three years earlier, the government had completed improvements on a trail from Valdez to Fairbanks that made wagon transport possible most of the year, and it was generally assumed that private capital should be used to finance railroad construction in the north. Despite numerous criticisms that existing roads were sufficient to meet current transportation needs in Alaska, that government funds could be put to better use elsewhere, and that Washington would be supporting socialism by constructing and operating a railroad, Congress approved a bill authorizing the expenditure of $35 million for a railroad in Alaska. Woodrow Wilson, who signed the bill on February 18, 1912, had previously voiced his approval of this measure in his first State of the Union message: "The construction of railways [in Alaska] is only the first step, is only thrusting in the key to the storehouse and throwing back the lock and opening the door. . . . We must use the resources of this country, not lock them up" (quoted in Gruening, 1954:177).[3] The Alaska Engineering Commission

3. For interesting notes concerning the congressional debate surrounding this issue, see Chapter 14 in Gruening (1954).

was assigned the responsibility of locating the best route from the interior to the southern coast, and in 1913, it presented two alternative routes to President Wilson—the first running from Cordova on the coast to Chitina, then on to Fairbanks, and the second beginning at Seward, then continuing through the Susitna Valley northward. Despite objections concerning issues of economic feasibility raised by Alaska's congressional delegate James Wickersham, Wilson chose the second route—from Seward to Fairbanks by way of Anchorage. The series of events that culminated in this choice determined the course of Alaskan history in several major ways. First, it established a pattern of federal spending in the territory contingent on possible gains to be realized through federal intervention. Construction of the railroad was premised on the belief that the nation, as a whole, would benefit from Alaska's resources, and when sufficient gains failed to materialize, federal attention—and appropriations— waned.

More specifically, by choosing the Seward-Fairbanks route, Wilson sealed the fate of the Cordova-Chitina region; the economic viability of this area fell markedly after the copper mines were depleted. Thus, the death of one community brought life to another by establishing Anchorage as the center of construction activities for the Alaska Railroad.[4] In the spring of 1915, about 2,000 workers and businessmen landed at the entrance to the Cook Inlet and quickly set up the rudiments of community life. By July, the town had been surveyed, and lots were auctioned to prospective buyers of all sorts: restaurant owners, lodging house operators, jewelers, tobacconists, druggists, painters, movers, barbers, tailors, blacksmiths, confectioners, contractors, dentists, doc-

4. It is not altogether clear why Anchorage (rather than Seward) was selected as the headquarters for railroad operations in Alaska. One account (Atwood, 1957) suggests that legal difficulties involving the purchase of the Alaska Northern Railroad and the surrounding areas of Seward convinced officials to opt for the Anchorage location. Others, however, are not convinced of this explanation, considering that the deep-water port of Seward was better than any found in the Cook Inlet. See Hunt (1976).

tors. Tents were slowly replaced by shanties of a more permanent nature, and two areas of the south end of the township were assigned special zoning uses: one for prostitutes, the other for European immigrant housing. At a town meeting held in August, residents voted to name the community "Anchorage" because of its strategic location in the territory. Bud Whitney, who was present at that meeting, reflected on their choice:

> We finally decided on Anchorage because it was the most significant. It really was an anchorage for the boats that brought freight to the railroad and to the mines. Boats would moor in the wide mouth of Ship Creek and unload onto barges. They did this until the dock was built in 1917, so the name really meant something. (quoted in Atwood [1957:9])

By early 1916, the population of Anchorage had tripled, making it the largest settlement in Alaska. This growth was mirrored by a corresponding increase in the social and cultural amenities available to community residents—churches, schools, movie theaters, hotels, a hospital, and a bank. What appeared as a boomtown in the making, however, ground to a halt the following year with the advent of the World War I. Railroad construction witnessed an immediate slowdown as materials and supplies increased in price and decreased in availability. The supply of labor dwindled when many from Anchorage were called into national service. (Over 75 percent of the men in town were subject to the draft.) As a result, the railroad was not finished until 1923 and only then with the help of two additional federal appropriations totalling $21 million.

Unfortunately, completion of the railroad did not bring renewed prosperity to Anchorage. Freight rates were not reduced, mining did not increase in profitability, and consequently Wilson's prediction that opening up the country would result in an influx of population failed to materialize. Angry residents complained that government land withdrawals precluded development of the interior and that private investors were waving the banner of conservation in an effort to ward off competition in the territory. Local resentment was fired as Congress, having already spent more than first anticipated, proved reluctant to fund the continuing operation of the line now that the railroad was complete.

Thus, on the eve of a national depression, it appeared that the early good fortune of Anchorage was to be short-lived as the prosperity of boom gave way to the decline of bust. By the beginning of the 1930s, the town's population had dropped to about 2,700, with one-third of the adult population out of work. The railroad had not been the gold mine that residents had hoped for (it was never to be a profitmaking enterprise), and yet another shot of federal assistance was required to revitalize the Anchorage economy.

Farming in the Matanuska Valley

As part of a national effort to assist farmers, the Matanuska Valley in south central Alaska was chosen as one of several sites for relocation of rural families under New Deal legislation. The colony, which was located fifty miles north of Anchorage, had at best a minimal impact on the population and economy of the area. It did, however, provide somewhat of a holding pattern for local residents between boomtime periods. More important, it was one of the few instances of federal involvement in the region that met with approval, rather than disdain, from Alaskans.

Attempts to develop the agricultural resources of Alaska, though incongruous with the popular conception of the state as a frozen wasteland, were not of recent origin. In 1898 money was appropriated to explore farming possibilities in the territory, and during the following five years, experimental stations were established throughout Alaska. Department of Agriculture reports described the prospects for agricultural production in glowing terms, but few residents from the continental United States responded. The reasons for this

poor response were obvious, for the same difficulties imped-
ing the development of other Alaskan resources hindered the
development of farming in the region. Long distances and
the high costs of freight drove the price of production
upward. Climate, even in the southern regions, was never a
certainty; one sharp frost meant economic disaster. Both a
viable market and sufficient local capital were lacking in the
sparsely populated territory, and, to complicate matters, economic competition was such that goods from Seattle were
less expensive than local products.

Prompted by the hardships suffered by midwestern farmers during the Depression, the federal government assumed
responsibility for what private enterprise had failed to support—the establishment of a profitable farming community in
south central Alaska. The Matanuska Valley Colony was the
most heavily publicized (and also the most romanticized);
journalists characterized the northern territory as a "safety
valve," as America's "last frontier" (*Time,* May 6, 1935, p.
17, cited by Hunt [1976:94–95]). For the 200 families and
400 unmarried laborers who came to Alaska in 1935,
however, the frontier did not look quite so promising. Although the settlers had been selected exclusively from other
northern states in an attempt to facilitate adaptation to the
Alaskan climate,[5] severe rains in May and June followed by
a cold and windy winter provided sufficient discouragement
to turn many families homeward. Problems of climate were
compounded by the variable quality of the soil, adjustments
to growing new crops, and the restricted distribution of
goods to the Anchorage area.

As a result of these and other difficulties, the Matanuska
farm project floundered for the next five years until construction of the military base at Fort Richardson began.
Although construction work meant an expanded market for
agricultural products, most of the settlers sought defense-re-
lated jobs, and farming failed to secure a significant place in

5. Members of the Matanuska Valley Colony were selected from
Michigan, Wisconsin, and Minnesota.

the Alaskan economy. This pattern has continued to the present, as virtually all of Anchorage's agricultural needs are met by outside producers. Rather than supporting rural farm production on a large scale, the Matanuska Valley has become a much sought-after residential location for upper-income suburbanites.

Despite these attempts to make rail transportation and agricultural production viable sectors of the local economy, the territory remained heavily dependent on external goods and services. In the decade prior to American involvement in World War II, Alaska was an American colony in many respects, and the center of colonial activity resided outside of Anchorage. Average annual out-shipments to the United States totalled $58.8 million in 1931 to 1940, while the average value of in-shipments was significantly less—$34.2 million—for the same period. Exports from Alaska were confined to a few products; canned salmon and gold accounted for over four-fifths of all out-shipments. On the other hand, imports to the territory were largely agricultural and manufactured goods (approximately 85 percent of all in-shipments), thus revealing the dependent nature of the local economy (Kresge, Morehouse, and Rogers, 1977:29).

The population of Alaska was concentrated in areas of specific resource production. Southeast Alaska, which accounted for the largest share of salmon, gold, fur, and timber exports, harbored almost half of the non-Native population when the 1939 census was taken. By contrast, the south central and interior regions of the territory contained only 27 percent and 17 percent of the non-Native population, respectively. The population of northwest Alaska, which had been the site of the turn-of-the-century gold rush, declined sharply with the passing of mining operations. Whereas Nome had been the largest city in Alaska in 1900, with a population of over 12,000, Juneau dominated the territorial landscape from 1920 to 1939. The combined populations of Fairbanks and Anchorage did not exceed the population of Juneau until the late 1930s. (See Table 2.1.)

Table 2.1. Population of Juneau, Fairbanks, and Anchorage as a Proportion of Alaska Population: 1920–1984

Year	Juneau Population	Percentage of State Population in Juneau	Fairbanks Population	Percentage of State Population in Fairbanks	Anchorage Population	Percentage of State Population in Anchorage	Total Alaska Population
1920*	5,893	10.7	2,182	4.0	1,856	3.4	55,036
1929	6,174	10.4	3,446	5.8	2,736	4.6	59,278
1939	8,563	11.8	5,692	7.6	4,229	5.8	72,524
1950	8,758	6.8	19,409	15.1	32,060	24.9	128,643
1960	9,745	4.3	43,412	19.2	82,833	36.6	226,167
1970	13,556	4.5	45,864	15.2	126,385	41.8	302,361
1980	19,528	4.9	53,983	13.4	174,431	43.4	401,851
1984†	23,729	4.5	64,186	12.3	243,829	46.6	523,048

*Data for 1920–1980 are from U.S. Bureau of the Census, *Census of Population,* 1920, 1929, 1939, 1950, 1960, 1970, 1980.
†Data from Alaska Department of Labor, *Alaska Population Overview,* September, 1985, p. 63.

During this same period, Alaska remained relatively impotent with regard to political decisionmaking. The second Organic Act of 1912 officially granted Alaska territorial status with the right to elect its own legislature, thereby granting a measure of local self-government to residents. But such a step was largely token in nature because the actions of this body were subject to U.S. congressional review. The scope and pervasiveness of federal involvement in Alaska were noted in a National Resources Planning Board report of 1941:

In many respects Alaska is a Federal province: the Governor is a Federal appointee, the law-enforcement and judicial system is administered by the United States Department of Justice, part of the local taxes are imposed by Act of Congress and collected by Federal officers, the fisheries and wildlife are under the jurisdiction of Federal and quasi-Federal agencies, about 98 percent of the land is in Federal ownership, the national defense program now changing the economic life of the Territory in a radical way is entirely in Federal control. This picture is remarkably different from the simple pattern of Federal activities that prevailed during territorial days in the [other] States. (quoted in Kresge, Morehouse, and Rogers, 1977:34)

In alluding to the radical changes under way in Alaska as a result of the war effort, the Planning Board report presaged the two major developments that would transform the economic and demographic composition of the territory. First, the dominant role of resource production in the economic life of the territory would be supplanted by that of U.S. government employment. Second, Anchorage would emerge from the war years as the primary center of economic and political activity in Alaska. The cycle of colonial dependence linking Alaska to the federal government would be replicated internally as the economic well-being of the territory became dependent on events in Anchorage.

The Military in Alaska

World War II restored economic vitality to Anchorage, and the military expenditures devoted to Alaska during this period were without precedent in the history of the territory. Talk of protecting territorial interests had surfaced in 1904 when Kiska Island in the Aleutians was reserved for a naval base. But there was no immediate threat at the time, and Kiska, as well as the rest of Alaska, remained undeveloped militarily. Thirty-five years passed before the federal government was convinced that Alaska was crucial to America's defense. Between 1941 and 1945, Congress appropriated over $1 billion for military development of the region. Most of this was spent in Anchorage, a community that entered the war a railroad town of less than 3,500 and emerged a military post with a population of over 11,000 (closer to 20,000 if those in the suburbs were included).

Construction of Fort Richardson and Elmendorf Air Force Base began in 1940. As might be expected, housing was in short supply for those who came seeking construction work. Overnight the high prices associated with the territory reappeared, only to be alleviated by assistance for housing construction under Federal Housing Administration legislation. Anchorage was booming again, and all of the characteristic signs of a rapidly expanding local economy—overcrowding, increased drinking and violence, a strain on city services— returned to south central Alaska. During these years, more than 150,000 members of the armed services passed through Anchorage. Like those involved in construction of the Alaska Railroad, the vast majority of them returned to the continental United States after a brief stay in Alaska. But in contrast to the temporary prosperity sparked by railroad construction, the effects of military construction in Anchorage would be felt long after the war. Total trade between Alaska and the United States not only had increased, but also was nearly balanced during the early 1940s. Prior to defense spending in Alaska, out-shipments from Alaska represented roughly two-thirds of all trade between the territory and the United States; for 1941 to 1942 they represented 47 percent of total trade.[6]

In addition to the construction of Fort Richardson, military expenditures provided for substantial improvements in the transportation system of Alaska through modernization of the railroad, expansion and upgrading of existing airfields, and construction of the AlCan Highway. Docks and wharves built by the army and coast guard during the war were released to the township of Anchorage as well.

The slowdown of military spending after the war might have resulted in yet another swing toward the "bust" side of Alaska's cyclical economy were it not for adoption of a Cold War policy by the United States toward the Soviet Union. Because of the region's proximity to the Arctic Circle, defense capabilities were intensified in Alaska through increases in appropriations and workforce. The Department of Defense spent approximately $350 million in the territory between 1949 and 1950, and the number of military personnel stationed in Alaska increased to 26,000 by the end of this period. Commercial development was quick to follow, as hotel and office buildings sprang up and air transportation services increased in availability. (By 1954, Anchorage was the fourth busiest center for air traffic operations in the United States.) Car registration in Anchorage rose 1,400 percent from 1940 to 1950, and school attendance increased ten times during this decade (Hunt, 1976:115). Anchorage was literally swelling to accommodate these newcomers, and for the first time, a stable population base was developing. By the time Alaska became a state in 1959, over one-third of all those living in the state would reside in Anchorage (see Table 2.1).

As the military presence in Alaska expanded during the 1940s and 1950s, resource development and production correspondingly declined. Canned salmon, which had averaged

6. These external trade statistics do not include military supplies and equipment, which were substantially greater than civilian goods. See Kresge, Morehouse, and Rogers (1977:35).

Table 2.2. Industrial Composition of Alaska's Total Employment Workforce: 1939–1958

Industry	1939		1950		1952		1958	
	(in thousands)	Percent	(in thousands)	Percent	(in thousands)	Percent	(in thousands)	Percent
Commodity Producing:								
Agriculture*	1.0	3.8	1.0	1.3	0.9	0.8	0.9	0.9
Fishing†	1.5	5.6	1.5	1.9	2.0	1.8	1.8	1.9
Mining								
Crude oil and gas	—	—	0.5	0.6	0.4	0.4	0.2	0.2
Other	4.5	16.9	1.4	1.8	1.3	1.2	0.9	0.9
Contract construction	1.3	4.9	6.3	8.1	10.3	9.2	5.1	5.3
Manufacturing								
Food products	4.2	15.8	4.7	6.0	4.7	4.2	3.0	3.1
Forest products	0.1	0.4	0.6	0.8	0.8	0.7	1.1	1.1
Other (including petroleum)	0.3	1.1	0.4	0.5	0.5	0.4	0.8	0.8
Total	12.9	48.5	16.4	21.0	20.9	18.7	13.8	14.4

Distributive Industries:
Transportation, communications, utilities

Air transportation	0.5	0.9	1.2	1.4	1.3	1.6	1.7
Other	1.5	2.8	3.6	3.1	2.8	4.1	4.3
Trade	2.5	4.9	6.3	6.7	6.0	6.6	6.9
Finance, insurance, real estate services, miscellaneous‡	1.4	4.6	5.9	6.1	5.5	8.1	8.4
Total	5.9	13.2	16.9	17.3	15.5	20.4	21.2
Government: Department of Defense§	0.6	32.0	41.0	57.5	51.5	42.5	44.3
Federal, non-defense	2.0	7.6	9.7	7.0	6.3	9.3	9.7
State (territory), local	1.0	2.1	2.7	2.5	2.2	5.0	5.2
Total	3.6	41.7	53.4	67.0	60.1	56.8	59.2
Unclassified ‖	4.2	6.8	8.7	6.4	5.7	5.0	5.2
TOTAL EMPLOYED WORKFORCE	26.6	78.1	100.0	111.6	100.0	96.0	100.0

Source: Kresge, David T., Thomas A. Morehouse, and George W. Rogers, *Issues in Alaska Development* (Seattle: University of Washington Press, 1977), pp. 38–39. Table appears courtesy of University of Washington Press. Percentage totals by industry reflect rounding within industry categories (in original).

* Includes agricultural wage and salary and unpaid family workers.

† Fishing employment substituted for Department of Labor estimate.

‡ Includes domestics.

§ Includes uniformed personnel and civilian employees of Department of Defense (Department of War and Navy in 1939).

‖ Self-employed and others.

6.9 million cases per year from 1934 to 1938, had fallen to an annual average of 2.8 million cases from 1954 to 1958. Gold production had averaged 589,000 ounces from 1933 to 1944; by 1954 to 1958 production had dropped in half to an average of 225,000 ounces. The industrial composition of the workforce reflected the shift to government-related activities (Table 2.2). From 1939 to 1958, employment in commodity producing industries had declined by 34 percent, while government employment had risen by 45 percent. The importance of defense expansion was even greater than these employment statistics suggest because construction employment and income were tied primarily to federal programs as well.

Defense expenditures began to decline in the mid-1950s, but in their wake they left many of the amenities found in urban areas elsewhere in the country. Had resource production remained the driving force in territorial affairs, these changes would undoubtedly have occurred more slowly. Government-related activities required a sustained workforce in contrast to mining and fishing industries, which were highly seasonal in nature. Concomitantly, families rather than young, single males began to migrate to Alaska, and the services that were available in other parts of the country followed closely behind. Despite these substantial improvements accompanying military and civilian government personnel to Alaska, Anchorage—and the rest of Alaska for that matter—still lacked a stable *economic* base. A strong push toward statehood was thought to be one step in achieving greater economic autonomy, but it was soon clear that governmental control of Alaskan lands precluded independent decisions regarding the use of the state's resources. In fact, a turn of bad luck soon after Alaska achieved statehood in 1959 demonstrated to Alaskans just how dependent on congressional benevolence they still were.

The Earthquake of 1964

On the eve of March 27, 1964, an earthquake measuring between 8.3 and 8.6 on the Richter scale struck Anchorage and the nearby towns of Valdez and Kodiak. Twice as intense as the San Francisco earthquake of 1906, the Good Friday quake devastated large portions of both residential and commercial sections of Anchorage. A total of 115 persons were killed in Alaska, although only nine lives were lost in the Anchorage area. Physical and ecological destruction, however, was far more severe. Exclusive of federal property, Anchorage suffered losses estimated between $200 million and $290 million in property damage, half of the damage for the entire state.[7] Salmon spawning beds were filled with silt, forests were uprooted, salt water flowed into freshwater lakes, and the nesting grounds of some birds were destroyed. Although they were now acting on behalf of a state rather than a territory, representatives from Alaska made the familiar trip to Washington with requests for federal disaster assistance. Millions of dollars poured into the state during the following two years in the form of home loan and mortgage programs, grants for urban renewal, and general expenditures for post-disaster relief.

The greatest increases in labor force participation occurred in the contract construction and government sectors. The number of construction workers rose by 55 percent in the month following the earthquake and continued to rise steadily throughout the remainder of the year. Personnel were needed to administer government relief programs, and as a result, federal civilian employment in Anchorage increased by over 6 percent during this same period, reversing a trend of alternating stability and decline that had characterized that sector for the past two years. Transportation, communication, trade, and service employment showed similar, though less dramatic, increases following the disaster. The total unemployment rate in Anchorage dropped from 8.8 percent in March to 7.3 percent in April, 1964.

Despite these positive effects realized by Anchorage as a consequence of federal assistance, the impact of disaster

7. These and subsequent statistics documenting the impact of the Anchorage earthquake are from Rogers (1970a; 1970b).

relief expenditures in the area was both minimal and short lived. The economy of Alaska had long depended on the destruction of property; in the previous two decades, this destruction had taken the form of the progressive obsolescence of military holdings. Transformation of Alaska from a proximate defense outpost against Japanese aggression in World War II to a long-range attack station as a check to Soviet military strength had necessitated construction of new facilities. Construction employment and per capita income had risen when this shift occurred, and the natural resource industries—fishing, timber, mining, oil—proceeded at about the same rate before and after the earthquake. As one economist noted, the most significant impact of the 1964 earthquake was the perpetuation of a debtor relationship between Alaska and the federal government:

> The State of Alaska was facing a critical financial period in its political development just before the earthquake. The federal transition funds and programs, designed to provide a gradual weaning of Alaska from its territorial dependence on the federal government, were to end that year. The disaster justified an extension of these programs and the state treasury emerged from the immediate pre-disaster period in much better financial shape than if there had been no earthquake. (Rogers, 1970a:75)

In such the same way that the Matanuska farming project eased regional economic instability in the 1930s, federal assistance following the Anchorage earthquake bought some time for Alaskans in the 1960s. They didn't have long to wait, for by the end of the decade, it was clear that the petroleum resources discovered on the North Slope would be the deciding factor in Alaskan economics for many years to come.

Oil on the North Slope

The Alaska many know best was born in the newspaper headlines of July 18, 1968, the day Atlantic Richfield and

Humble Oil announced the discovery of oil reserves at Prudhoe Bay. In less than two months, the State of Alaska auctioned off 450,000 acres of the bay (containing an estimated 10 billion barrels of oil) for a total amount in excess of $900 million. Host to the largest petroleum lease sale in U.S. history, the forty-ninth state became the immediate focus of national attention. Alaskans in general were pleased, for the development of Alaska's resources meant new construction, and that, of course, meant new jobs. Their enthusiasm faded quickly, however, because announcement of plans to begin construction of the pipeline in June, 1969, were quickly followed by the realization that *construction in* Alaska did not necessarily translate into *jobs for* Alaskans. There were plenty of Americans who expected to share these new employment opportunities with their northern neighbors, and it was this sizable group of newcomers in search of pipeline fortunes that would later intensify Alaskans' dislike of "Outsiders."

As it turned out, Alaskans and Outsiders alike were prematurely optimistic about construction opportunities on the North Slope. Recent passage of the National Environmental Policy Act necessitated completion of an environmental impact statement before work on the pipeline could begin. Conservationists who opposed construction of the pipeline had several strong arguments to their credit: the environs of numerous wild animals would be disturbed, and the patterns of caribou migration would be diverted by the pipeline, thus affecting native subsistence hunting. Oil spills into Alaska's rivers and streams were a possibility, and tanker accidents could cripple the fishing industry along the state's coast. Of even greater consequence, the proposed port terminal at the south end of the pipeline was Valdez, one of the villages levelled in the earthquake of 1964. Alaskans who had witnessed that event feared that another quake might precipitate an uncontrolled flow of crude oil into the seas of south central Alaska.

In the face of these objections, legislative debate gave way to increasing fears of a national energy crisis. The Senate approved a bill authorizing pipeline construction by a narrow margin of 50 to 49, but the measure met with little resistance in the House. Nearly six years after the discovery of oil at Prudhoe Bay, work on the pipeline began in April, 1974. The effects of increased population and corresponding service demands were felt immediately in Alaska, with the major impact realized in Fairbanks and Valdez. But because of massive doses of federal assistance during the military build-up of the 1940s and 1950s, Anchorage was to reap many of the benefits resulting from oil development on the North Slope. It was the logical choice for the state headquarters of the oil companies; the support facilities offered by Fairbanks at the time were minor by comparison. And an expansion of state agencies necessary for pipeline development would merely be an additional step in a previously established trend of making Anchorage the largest center of government in the state. These indirect benefits accruing to Anchorage as a consequence of the pipeline were a source of good fortune, for when the immediate effects of the pipeline (e.g., construction employment) had passed, activity in the tertiary sectors of the Alaskan economy would continue to expand.

Regardless of the nature of these effects, the changes witnessed by Anchorage at the onset of pipeline construction were striking. There were signs of expansion everywhere. The most visible indication of change was the 16 percent increase in population between July, 1974, and July, 1975, bringing the total population of Anchorage to nearly 178,000. (This represented a 41 percent increase in population over the 126,000 figure of 1970.) Parallel trends were apparent in other areas of community life. After a 29 percent decrease in the number of building permits authorized in the previous year, permits issued in 1974 showed an increase of 35 percent, and an additional jump of 42 percent in 1975. In February, 1974, the unemployment rate had risen to a new high of 9.8 percent; by August, 1975, it had dropped to a low of 4.5 percent. As expected, the largest increase in employment occurred in the trade and service sectors, which boasted an increase of 5.1 percent during this two-year period.

Local service facilities were feeling the strain of increased demand as well. In 1973, 126,114 vehicles were registered and the next year 181,349, a change of 44 percent. Hospital admissions were up 79 percent in the same period, whereas the number of physicians practicing in Anchorage increased by 25 percent. During 1974 to 1975, the number of passengers and the amount of freight transported through the Anchorage International Airport rose 17 percent and 42 percent, respectively, and the tonnage received at the docks expanded by 28 percent. Although the pipeline provided a substantial boost in transport levels for both Anchorage and Fairbanks, in Fairbanks its effects were realized in a sharp increase followed by a steady decline in post-pipeline years. In Anchorage, increases in transport levels were more moderate and continued into future years (Figures 2.1 and 2.2).

Yet, statistics are not what local residents remember when they discuss the pipeline today. What made a lasting impression on the minds of most was that the pipeline brought crime and high prices to Alaska. Certainly, neither crime nor high prices were anything new to the state, but the rapid influx of newcomers exacerbated previous conditions and the resulting instability provided fodder for national media reports concerning Alaska in the mid-1970s. Although the crime rate did not increase in proportion to the population during this period, the percentage of particular offenses committed in Anchorage rose substantially: assault, 16 percent; robbery, 65 percent; burglary, 17 percent; grand larceny, 45 percent; and auto theft, 52 percent. The prices for local goods and services displayed similar dramatic increases, as the consumer price index rose by 10.8 percent in 1974 and 13.7 percent in 1975. (Previous and subsequent annual increases in the consumer price index were somewhere between 3 and 4 percent.) The largest contribution to the increase in prices came from the cost of housing. "Pipeline apartments" sprang up everywhere, and it was not uncommon to find even the smallest one-bedroom renting for over $500.

Figure 2.1 Passenger Traffic, Anchorage and Fairbanks International Airports: 1973–1980

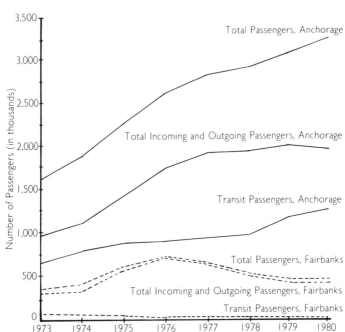

Source: Alaska Transportation Consultants and Dupere and Associates, *International Airport Study for Anchorage and Fairbanks,* Anchorage, AK., December, 1980.

By the end of the decade, construction of the trans-Alaska pipeline—and the changes it brought to Anchorage—was old news. Population had fluctuated somewhat during the post-pipeline years, but Anchorage retained over 40 percent of the state population (nearly 175,000).[8] Unemployment had levelled off at about 7.0 percent, and despite the fact that

8. Compare this with the pattern of population growth and decline witnessed by Fairbanks before and after the pipeline construction: 1970, 45,000; 1976, 70,000; 1978, 59,000; and 1980, 54,000.

Figure 2.2. Freight Traffic, Anchorage and Fairbanks International Airports: 1973–1980

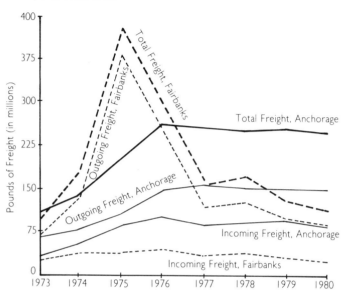

Source: Alaska Transportation Consultants and Dupere and Associates, *International Airport Study for Anchorage and Fairbanks,* Anchorage, AK., December, 1980.

Anchorage was still the most expensive place in the country to live, local prices were increasing at roughly the same rate across the nation. Things were beginning to slow down once again, and Anchorage was faced with an oversupply of construction projects left in the wake of the pipeline. Empty office space, apartments, and condominiums meant a renter's market, and that same one-bedroom apartment that went for $525 a month in the summer of 1975 could be had for $395 a month, with half a month's rent free if a six-month lease was signed. Nevertheless, few Anchorage residents were pessimistic about the future of the local economy because there was widespread speculation concerning renewed prosperity as a result of two pending projects—construction of the natural gas pipeline and the sale of oil leases in the Beaufort Sea. The major role played by Anchorage in the contemporary affairs of Alaska guaranteed that future developments anywhere in the state would be felt in their community.

Metropolitan Dominance in Alaska

The institutional developments that gave birth to the dominance of Anchorage in this century have transformed the landscape of Alaska. Their most obvious consequence has been the increasing urbanization of Alaska. At the close of World War I, the territory had only one town (Juneau) with a population greater than 2,500, representing an urban population of less than 6 percent of the total state population. Over the following five decades, the urban population roughly doubled each ten years, until by 1970 over half of all Alaskans were living in urban areas. The decade between 1970 and 1980, however, marked a significant change in this pattern of growth. Although the proportion of state residents living in urban areas continued to increase (from 56.9 percent to 64.3 percent), the decennial census of 1980 registered a *decrease* in the number of urban places (from 15 to 13). At the same time, the number of rural places increased dramatically.

The major implications of this pattern of settlement are two-fold. First, the settlement of Alaska has proceeded in the direction of urban primacy, in which a single major metropolitan center has come to dominate the surrounding hinterlands of the region. In this regard the development of Alaska parallels that of Australia, where a disproportionate number of persons are found in Melbourne and Sydney.[9]

9. The settlement patterns of Alaska and Australia are similar in other respects. For example, both display migration patterns of relocation from one city to another, rather than from city to bush areas. They both have engendered a system of urban hierarchies and regional competition, a topic to be considered shortly. For documentation of settlement in Australia, see Alexander (1947), Winks (1971), and Bourne and Logan (1976).

Thus, whereas the population density of Alaska was less than one person per square mile in 1980, that of the Anchorage borough exceeded 100 persons per square mile. With all urban areas combined, the state harbored a greater percentage of persons living in urban areas than that in twenty-two other states.[10]

Second, economic and political activity that was once distributed among major population centers has been concentrated in Anchorage. With the decline of gold and timber production in southeast Alaska, the population of Juneau decreased steadily from 1920 to the present. The increase in population witnessed by Fairbanks as a result of military construction secured its position as the second largest city in Alaska, but at no point after the war was Fairbanks more than half the size of Anchorage. As the economy moved from resource production to service and trade industries, the focus of economic activity shifted from Juneau and Fairbanks to Anchorage.

After the initial build-up of military Alaska, there was very little competition among these centers in either trade or service sectors of the territorial-state economy (Tables 2.3 to 2.5). In both the number of establishments and sales as a proportion of state totals, retail and wholesale trade declined in Juneau from 1948 to 1982. Fairbanks sustained a relatively constant percentage of Alaskan trade, fluctuating somewhere between 12 and 14 percent during this period. Anchorage, on the other hand, contained over one-third of all retail establishments and over one-half of all wholesale establishments by 1982. More than half of both retail and

10. The states reported by the U.S. Census Bureau as having fewer persons living in areas of 2,500 or more in 1980 were Indiana, 64.2 percent; Wisconsin, 64.2 percent; Nebraska, 62.9 percent; Wyoming, 62.7 percent; Georgia, 62.4 percent; New Mexico, 61.8 percent; Tennessee, 60.4 percent; Alabama, 60.0 percent; Iowa, 58.6 percent; South Carolina, 54.1 percent; Idaho, 54.0 percent; Montana, 52.9 percent; New Hampshire, 52.2 percent; Arkansas, 51.6 percent; Kentucky, 50.9 percent; North Dakota, 48.8 percent; North Carolina, 48.0 percent; Maine, 47.5 percent; Mississippi, 47.3 percent; South Dakota, 46.4 percent; West Virginia, 36.2 percent; Vermont, 33.8 percent.

Table 2.3. Number of Establishments and Total Sales in Retail Trade: Alaska, Anchorage, Fairbanks, Juneau, 1948–1982

| | | Number of Establishments | | | | | |
| | | Anchorage | | Fairbanks | | Juneau | |
Year	Alaska Number	Number	Percent	Number	Percent	Number	Percent
1948*	1,311	208	15.9	121	9.2	116	8.8
1954	1,510	339	22.5	169	11.2	117	7.7
1958	1,659	423	25.5	234	14.1	98	5.9
1963	1,607	386	24.0	208	12.9	94	5.8
1967	1,957	720	36.8	239	12.2	127	6.5
1972†	2,972	1,172	39.4	410	13.8	139	4.7
1977	3,781	1,426	37.7	537	14.2	192	5.1
1982	4,579	1,838	40.1	607	13.3	268	5.9

*Data for 1948–1967 are from U.S. Bureau of the Census, *Census of Business: Retail Trade, Area Statistics*, 1948, 1954, 1958, 1963, 1967.

†Data for 1972–1982 are from U.S. Bureau of the Census, *Census of Retail Trade, Area Statistics*, 1972, 1977, 1982.

Table 2.4. Number of Establishments and Total Sales in Wholesale Trade: Alaska, Anchorage, Fairbanks, Juneau, 1948–1982

| | | Number of Establishments | | | | | |
| | | Anchorage | | Fairbanks | | Juneau | |
Year	Alaska Number	Number	Percent	Number	Percent	Number	Percent
1948*	111	13	11.7	7	6.3	13	11.7
1954	184	53	28.8	24	13.0	9	4.9
1958	254	102	40.2	31	12.2	14	5.5
1963	291	121	41.6	44	15.1	18	6.2
1967	365	179	49.0	47	12.9	21	5.8
1972‡	506	259	51.2	80	15.8	29	5.7
1977	649	377	58.1	96	14.8	25	3.9
1982	706	413	58.5	95	13.5	25	3.5

*Data for 1948–1967 are from U.S. Bureau of the Census, *Census of Business: Wholesale Trade, Area Statistics*, 1948, 1954, 1958, 1963, 1967.

†Not available from Census records.

‡Data for 1972–1982 are from U.S. Bureau of the Census, *Census of Wholesale Trade, Area Statistics*, 1972, 1977, 1982.

(Table 2.3, con't.)

	Sales ($1,000)						
	Anchorage		Fairbanks		Juneau	
Alaska $	$	Percent	$	Percent	$	Percent
96,748	29,323	30.3	17,450	18.0	8,605	8.9
174,514	57,542	33.0	31,258	17.9	12,170	7.0
202,038	73,963	36.6	39,762	19.7	11,777	5.8
284,408	115,023	40.4	50,084	17.6	19,572	6.9
402,516	207,586	51.6	65,590	11.3	26,748	6.6
772,125	427,049	55.3	115,096	14.9	43,783	5.7
1,830,668	962,140	52.6	320,011	17.5	82,523	4.5
3,227,327	1,794,843	55.6	426,349	13.2	172,785	5.4

(Table 2.4, con't.)

	Sales ($1,000)						
	Anchorage		Fairbanks		Juneau	
Alaska $	$	Percent	$	Percent	$	Percent
32,216	5,790	18.0	—†	—	5,179	16.1
94,721	40,505	42.8	—	—	5,892	6.2
137,942	74,804	54.2	19,201	13.9	5,654	4.1
180,605	94,722	52.4	29,692	16.4	10,397	5.8
286,063	179,467	62.7	42,994	15.0	8,152	2.8
604,125	378,284	62.6	69,061	11.4	18,957	3.1
1,562,699	981,821	62.8	238,342	15.3	45,879	2.9
2,737,328	1,885,672	68.9	299,821	11.0	72,035	2.6

Table 2.5. Number of Establishments and Receipts in Service Industries: Alaska, Anchorage, Fairbanks, Juneau, 1948–1982

Number of Establishments

Year	Alaska Number	Anchorage Number	Anchorage Percent	Fairbanks Number	Fairbanks Percent	Juneau Number	Juneau Percent
1948*	243	56	23.0	33	13.6	41	16.9
1954	694	176	25.4	128	18.4	42	6.1
1958	875	224	25.6	123	14.1	54	6.2
1963	1,050	300	28.6	145	13.8	45	4.3
1967	1,530	708	46.3	203	13.3	99	6.5
1972†	2,801	1,515	54.1	422	15.1	144	5.1
1977	4,352	2,253	51.8	672	15.4	226	5.2
1982	2,587‡	1,490	57.6	327	12.6	165	6.4

*Data for 1948–1967 are from U.S. Bureau of the Census, *Census of Business: Service Industries, Area Statistics,* 1948, 1954, 1958, 1963, 1967.

†Data for 1972–1982 are from U.S. Bureau of the Census, *Census of Service Industries, Area Statistics,* 1972, 1977, 1982.

‡Changes in the Census classification of service industries reduces the count of number of establishments in 1982.

wholesale sales for the same year were realized in Anchorage. A similar pattern is evident in the distribution of service industries and receipts for this period.[11]

Supporting documentation for the economic superiority of Anchorage is found in employment statistics. With the exception of resource-producing and manufacturing industries, approximately half—or more than half—of each industrial classification in Alaska is composed of persons working in Anchorage (Table 2.6). Notable among these many industries

11. Newcomers to Alaska become aware that Anchorage is the dominant service community in the state the moment they pick up the local phone directory. In recent directories yellow page listings outnumber white page listings by roughly five to one.

(Table 2.5, con't.)

	Receipts ($1,000)					
	Anchorage		Fairbanks		Juneau	
Alaska $	$	Percent	$	Percent	$	Percent
4,646	2,140	46.1	736	15.8	589	12.7
20,234	8,248	40.8	3,650	18.0	1,585	7.8
28,442	11,156	39.2	5,502	19.3	2,069	7.3
45,480	19,000	41.8	5,345	11.8	2,770	6.1
67,219	40,219	59.8	8,211	12.2	3,865	5.7
175,731	110,233	62.7	25,442	14.5	11,067	6.3
513,843	329,137	64.1	73,353	14.3	22,368	4.4
1,154,916	795,264	68.9	129,407	11.2	56,913	4.9

is the overwhelming concentration of finance, insurance, and real estate employment in Anchorage. Banking employment, which constitutes the largest portion of this sector, exceeds both state and national averages. The banks in Anchorage are also the largest in the state; their combined assets account for approximately four-fifths of all assets of Alaskan banks (Figure 2.3).

As Table 2.6 documents, government continues to be a major employer in Alaska. Although only 15 percent of the Anchorage workforce was composed of public administrators in 1980, nearly half of all government employees in Alaska worked in Anchorage. There has, however, been a shift in the composition of the government workforce in the last twenty years (Table 2.7). At the time of statehood about one-third of all government employees worked for state and local governments. By the end of the 1960s, that number had reached 50 percent and increased rapidly in the following decade. Federal civilian employment, by contrast, remained

Table 2.6. Employment by Major Industry Group For Persons 16 Years Old and Over, Alaska and Anchorage, 1980

	Alaska		Anchorage		
Industry	Number	Percent	Number	Percent	Percent of State
Agriculture, forestry, fisheries, mining	9,817	6.0	3,627	4.7	37.0
Construction	13,127	8.0	6,146	7.9	46.8
Manufacturing (durable and non-durable goods)	10,349	6.3	2,450	3.2	23.7
Transportation	12,305	7.5	6,309	8.1	51.3
Communications and other public utilities	6,085	3.7	2,994	3.9	49.2
Wholesale trade	4,100	2.5	2,775	3.6	67.7
Retail trade	24,870	15.1	12,606	16.2	50.7
Finance, insurance, and real estate	8,384	5.1	5,942	7.6	70.9
Business and repair services	6,346	3.8	3,577	4.6	56.4
Personal, entertainment and recreation services	7,212	4.4	3,787	4.9	52.5
Professional and related services	36,027	21.9	15,745	20.2	43.7
Public administration	26,252	15.9	11,796	15.2	44.9
TOTAL LABOR FORCE	164,874	100.2*	77,754	100.1*	47.2

Source: U.S. Bureau of the Census, *Census of Population: Detailed Population Characteristics*, 1980.

*Percentage totals reflect rounding within industry categories.

Figure 2.3.   Total Assets (in thousands of dollars), Anchorage and All
Alaskan Banks for First Quarter: 1977–1982

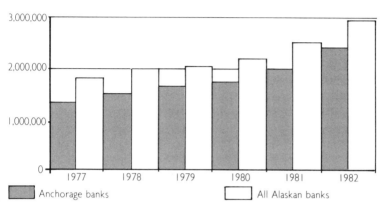

Anchorage banks   All Alaskan banks

Source: Research Design Productions, *The Anchorage Factbook—1983*
(Anchorage, AK.: Research Design Productions, 1983). Based on Alaska State
Department of Commerce and Economic Development, Division of Banking,
Securities, Small Loans, and Corporations data.

relatively constant at just over 17,000 during this same
period. Thus, although the presence of government continues
to be felt in Alaskan economic affairs, it has increasingly
become a role played by state and local entities. This growth
at the non-federal level may be traced directly to the management of the state's petroleum resources: the lease sales at
Prudhoe Bay, construction of the trans-Alaska pipeline, and
the more recent increases in oil revenues and state spending
in the early 1980s (Kresge, Morehouse, Rogers, 1977).

   As the center for economic and political activity in Alaska,
Anchorage has assumed a position similar to that of the
federal government as the core influence in the state. It is
the vital link between the continental United States and the
rest of Alaska, the gate through which information, capital,
and population pass both into and out of the state. The
dominance of Anchorage in contemporary Alaskan affairs

Table 2.7. Government Employment in Alaska: 1961–1981 (in thousands)

Year	Federal Civilian	State	Local	State and Local Total	Total Government	Percent of State and Local of Total
1961*	15.6	4.6	3.6	8.2	23.8	34.5
1962	15.7	5.2	4.1	9.3	25.0	37.2
1963	16.6	6.2	4.4	10.5	27.1	38.7
1964	17.3	6.3	4.5	10.8	28.1	38.4
1965	17.4	7.0	5.2	12.2	29.6	41.2
1966	17.5	7.7	5.7	13.4	30.9	43.4
1967	17.4	8.1	6.3	14.4	31.8	45.3
1968	16.9	8.7	6.6	15.3	32.2	46.6
1969	16.5	9.3	7.5	16.9	33.4	50.6
1970†	17.1	10.4	8.1	18.5	35.6	52.0

Year						
1971	17.3	11.7	9.0	20.7	38.0	54.5
1972	17.2	13.3	10.0	23.3	40.5	57.5
1973	17.2	13.8	10.6	24.6	41.8	58.9
1974	18.0	14.2	11.6	25.8	43.8	58.9
1975	18.3	15.5	13.3	28.8	47.1	61.1
1976	17.9	14.1	15.2	29.3	47.2	62.1
1977	17.7	13.9	17.2	31.1	48.8	63.7
1978	18.1	14.3	19.8	34.3	52.4	65.5
1979	17.9	15.0	21.6	36.6	54.5	67.2
1980	17.8	15.4	20.9	36.3	54.1	67.1
1981‡	17.7	16.6	22.9	39.5	57.2	69.1

*Data for 1961–1969 from Kresge, David T., Thomas A. Morehouse, and George W. Rogers, *Issues in Alaska Development* (Seattle: University of Washington Press, 1977), p. 50.

†Data for 1970–1980 from Institute of Social and Economic Research, University of Alaska, Anchorage.

‡Data for 1981 from U.S. Department of Labor, Bureau of Labor Statistics, *Employment and Earnings, States and Areas, 1977–81*, September, 1982.

has forged the link between urbanization and continued economic vitality in the state, a realization made by a recent governor of Alaska as he spoke of the options available to newcomers to the state today: /

> It's pretty hard to come from elsewhere and choose to live in the bush, and actually move into an area in which there isn't any viable economy. . . . You don't have the homestead programs where the availability of land is readily acquired. You don't have the capability to go out and trap, for example, to quote "live off the land" unquote, in a manner in which we did then. Simply, the economics preclude it, plus the fact that most people [who] have the dream of going out and living off the land [find that] the land gets to taste pretty crummy after a few months of trying to live on it, subsist in it. (Hammond, 1979)

The governor speaks for many Alaskans, who, although having been forced to acknowledge the regional supremacy of Anchorage, are nevertheless displeased by the currents shaping Alaska today. The ascendance of Anchorage in the landscape of Alaska seems but an extension of the exploitation of peripheral by core regions experienced under federal control in territorial days. Although the role of "Outsiders" in Alaskan affairs has long been a source of antagonism for Alaskans, today residents of Fairbanks and Juneau voice a similar complaint when they refer to Anchorage as Alaska's "American city." In both real and metaphorical terms, Anchorage is the core of contemporary Alaska.

CHAPTER 3

A Second Home:
Anchorage as a Community of Migrants

The history of Alaska is a repetitive saga of economic and political dependency of the region on the federal government, but there is a more fundamental link between Alaska and the rest of the country: the people who live there. Most Alaskans have known a life elsewhere, a fact not without consequence for those who make Anchorage their home.

Alaska is a land of migrants. Few living there today were born in Alaska; fewer still will remain in the state until they die. In fact, those who stay for longer than a dozen years may well be recognized as old-timers by most local residents. Although the process of internal migration contributes to the shifting landscape of every state, it wields exceptional power in Alaska. At the taking of the 1980 census, only slightly over 30 percent of the people living in Alaska were natives of the state. This proportion represented less than half of the national average for 1980 nativity; compared with the other states and the District of Columbia, Alaska ranked forty-ninth in the proportion of native born. This comparison is even more marked in the case of Anchorage, where only about one resident out of five (22.2 percent) was born in Alaska.

Not only does Alaska have few residents native to the state, but it also has rapid turnover. Nearly one-third (31.5 percent) of Alaskans who were five years and older in 1980 lived outside of the state in 1975, a figure almost three times the United States average of 11.6 percent (U.S. Department of Commerce, 1983). Compared with other states, Alaska was second only to Nevada (34.2 percent) in proportion of recently arrived population. In Anchorage the proportion of persons changing residence was even higher (36.1 percent). The fluidity of the Anchorage population is further reflected in municipal surveys that report the average length of residence to be less than ten years (Ender, 1979).

Of what significance are these indicators of geographic mobility among Anchorage residents? The first and most obvious consequence is that they, like all migrants, have ties to other places. No matter how long ago the move occurred, the biographies of Anchorage residents include experiences linked to another time and place. For most of them, a part of the self is lodged elsewhere in the continental United States.[1] Thus, the move to Alaska is accurately illustrated in the metaphor of a move from geographic core to periphery—a redistribution of the population within the boundaries of the nation. Phrased in denominational terms, most Anchorage residents were Americans long before they became Alaskans.

Yet at the same time that the migrant status of Alaskans attaches them to other Americans, it also fosters their sense of difference from others. Because they have had a home outside of Alaska, their current experiences in Alaska are measured against some prior standard of comparison. Thus, the role of Alaskans is born out of comparison to non-Alaskans. Although many can lay claim to being Americans, few can call themselves Alaskans. By simple virtue of having moved to Alaska, residents of the state can point to a characteristic that few share.

In large part, this process of differentiation is possible because of the distant and non-contiguous location of Alaska from the rest of the nation. It is unlikely that Anchorage residents will interact frequently with persons living in the continental United States, just as it is reasonable to expect that few of them will ever visit Alaska. Although it should

1. Foreign immigration continues to play an insignificant role in the settlement of Alaska. Only 2.4 percent of those living in Alaska in 1980 had been living abroad in 1975. The comparable figure for Anchorage was 2.9 percent.

come as no surprise to find that both groups rely on stereotypical views of one another (cf. LeVine and Campbell, 1972; Brewer and Campbell, 1976), the process of stereotyping is fundamentally different for Alaskans and Outsiders. Because the vast majority of Alaskans have lived in other parts of the country, their view of their current location is shaped by comparative experiences. Non-residents, on the other hand, do not have a similar set of experiences that might serve as a backdrop for their perceptions of Alaskans. This difference is not trivial, for it means that Alaskans are more likely to see themselves as part of a national system than are other Americans.

Understanding Anchorage as a community of migrants, then, requires that migration to Alaska be analyzed in terms of two dimensions, one structural and one symbolic. This chapter examines the relationship between these two dimensions by comparing the structural location of Alaska within a system of internal migration with the resulting symbolic response of Alaskans to their location in that system. Because the overwhelming majority of migrants to Alaska come from other American communities, the differentials that account for migration elsewhere in the country should be equally powerful in explaining migration to Anchorage. Any deviation from national patterns of selectivity might be explained by the distance of Alaska from the continental United States. And because migrants have made a life in other parts of the country, one would expect the identities of migrants as Alaskan residents to be forged out of a comparison with previous community experience. In making this comparison, Anchorage residents define a unique, and decidedly more favorable, position for Alaskans within the hierarchy of American cultural values.

Migration Differentials

Numerous investigations have focused on the factors descriptive of those most likely to relocate, and despite the diversity of the setting that characterizes this research, the findings have been relatively consistent. Thus, for example, new work continues to support the well-documented finding that age varies inversely with the propensity to migrate. Adding to this a number of other group traits, we have arrived at a rather well-accepted list of characteristics describing those most likely to move: young, white, male, well educated, and employed in white-collar occupations.

If migrants to Alaska were representative of others moving within the nation, then we would expect them to share these traits.[2] Such a comparison between Alaskan newcomers and other mobile Americans bears out this expectation with one important qualification: the distance of Alaska as a potential destination for migrants. If the probability of moving decreases as the distance between points of origin and destination increases (Stouffer, 1940, 1960; Ravenstein, 1885; Wadycki, 1974), then Alaska would appear to be an unlikely destination for most American migrants. Considering other possible moves, Alaska will likely represent the most distant destination. What characteristics, then, would one expect migrants to Alaska to possess? How does the distance of move affect these differentials of selectivity?

The answer to these questions requires viewing not only migrants in relation to non-migrants, but also *distant* movers in relation to movers in general. Put differently, previous research demonstrates that within the migrant pool, those of comparatively higher education and occupational status and those of majority group membership are more likely to move farther when they move (Courchene, 1970; McInnis, 1971; Rose, 1970). Hence, migrants to Alaska should share the

2. The 1979 Anchorage survey data do not allow for a strict test of these migration differentials because they do not include a group of non-migrants with which respondents might be compared. Nevertheless, on the basis of previous research to establish a standard for comparison, modal characteristics of Alaskan migrants might then be viewed in relation to these findings. This allows for a description of movement to Alaska in the larger context of U.S. internal migration.

characteristics of other migrants but to a greater degree. A brief examination of several migration differentials confirms this expectation (see Table 3.1).[3]

Age. One of the most consistent findings of research exploring migration differentials is that those who move tend to be in their late teens, twenties, or early thirties (Browning and Feindt, 1969; Hamilton, 1964; Shryrock, 1964; Thomas, 1958; U.S. Department of Commerce, Bureau of the Census, 1978). Explanations for this result address the willingness of younger persons to take advantage of opportunities found elsewhere and to adjust easily to new surroundings once they have moved. This pattern of age selectivity corresponds to data from the Anchorage sample, as almost two-thirds of the sample moved to Alaska in their late teens or twenties.[4]

Education. Previous research indicates that better-educated persons are more likely to be aware of opportunities available to them in other places and, consequently, are more likely to migrate than are those with less education (Bogue, 1969; Lansing and Mueller, 1967; Long, 1973). Most migrants to Anchorage have completed some college, as reflected in the high mean and median values of education.

---

3. Unless otherwise noted, the data presented in this and subsequent chapters are from a random survey of 134 Anchorage households completed in 1979. Verbatim quotations from respondents in the sample are identified by sex, age, occupation, and length of residence in Alaska. (See Appendices for details of this research.) Migrants are defined as those who were not born in Alaska or who did not move to the state with parent or guardian. Respondents who meet either of these requirements constitute 79 percent (n=105) of the Anchorage survey sample.

4. There is reason to believe that migration to Anchorage follows an age pattern that has predominated in the United States for many years. Research concerning those moving west in the nineteenth century reveals that the largest group of migrants comprised young males (Billington, 1974; Riegel, 1956; Thernstrom and Knights, 1970). Thus, frontier migration appears to be a subset of a national pattern of geographic mobility (Lee, 1961).

Table 3.1. Characteristics of Migrants in the 1979 Anchorage Sample*

Characteristic	Percent	Number	Characteristic	Percent	Number
Sex:			Occupation:		
Male	69.5		Professional,		
Female	30.5		managerial	26.4	
	100.0	(105)	Technical, adminis-		
			trative support	24.1	
Race:			Service	10.3	
White	95.2		Farming, fishing,		
Black	4.8		forestry	1.1	
	100.0	(105)	Precision produc-		
			tion, draft and		
Marital Status:			repair	8.0	
Married	75.2		Operators, laborers	13.8	
Divorced	10.5		Armed services	16.1	
Separated	3.8			99.9	(87)
Widowed	1.9				
Never married	8.6		Age at Time of Move:		
	100.0	(105)	16–24	40.8	
			25–29	23.3	
Education:			30 or older	35.9	
Less than high				100.0	(103)
school diploma	4.8				
High school			Mean—28 years		
diploma	27.6		Median—26 years		
Some college	30.5				
College degree			Length of Residence		
or more	37.1		in Alaska:		
	100.0	(105)	Less than 5 years	36.2	
			5–9 years	22.8	
Mean—14.6 years			10–19 years	23.9	
Median—14.3 years			20 years or more	17.1	
				100.0	(105)
			Mean—10.06 years		
			Median—6.88 years		

*Respondents in the Anchorage survey who were born in Alaska or who moved to Alaska with parent or guardian are excluded from these frequencies.

Occupation. The argument for differential selectivity based on occupational status assumes that positions requiring technical or skilled competencies attract potential migrants from greater distances, whereas the demand for unskilled labor may be met locally. Hence, persons in white-collar occupations are more likely to move than those in blue-collar occupations. It is not surprising to find that the majority of migrants in the Anchorage survey worked in professional-technical or managerial positions when they moved, given the service-oriented nature of the Anchorage economy.

Race. Minority group members are thought to move less frequently than those of the majority (Lansing and Mueller, 1967; Shaw, 1975; Shryrock, 1964). Although researchers agree on this point, their explanations for this finding vary (Ritchey, 1976). Some maintain that the characteristics that distinguish migrants from non-migrants (e.g., occupation, education, and age) are the same for majority and minority groups. It is only because members of minority groups have proportionately less education and work in lower-status occupations that they are less likely to migrate. An alternate view suggests that minority group status exerts an independent effect on the probability of migration. Here, others have argued that minorities are less willing to leave friends and family members. The extremely small numbers of blacks in the sample suggests similarities between migration to Alaska and migration elsewhere in the country.

To review and summarize these characteristics of Alaskan migrants is to describe them as a group of "chronic movers" (Morrison, 1971; Miller, 1977; Long, 1973), a subset of Americans who account for a disproportionate share of internal migration. Further support for this conclusion is found in tracing the migration histories of respondents in the Anchorage sample, for in doing so, the temporary nature of their stay in Alaska is brought into greater relief.

Migration Histories

In addition to age, education, and other social characteristics, a number of other factors have been correlated with migration outcomes. For example, knowing the number of times a person has moved in the past allows us to better predict whether that person will move in the future (Goldstein, 1964; Morrison, 1971; Rogers, 1968). That is, the effects of migration appear to be cumulative: the more often a person changes residences, the more likely he or she is to move again. Compared with other Americans, Anchorage residents have lived in a greater number of places (Table 3.2). As one would expect, the principal differences between these

Table 3.2. Number of Residences: Anchorage Survey and Comparable National Data

Number of Residences	Anchorage* (Percent)	United States† (Percent)
One	7.5	26.5
Two	29.9	29.1
Three	18.7	19.7
Four	17.2	10.6
Five	7.5	5.6
Six or more	19.3	8.5
Total	100.1	100.0
Mean	3.65	—
Median	3.18	2.3

*n=134. The entire sample is included here to allow for comparability with the national data.

†Source: Taeuber, Karl E., Leonard Chiazze, Jr., and William Haenszel, *Migration in the United States: An Analysis of Residence Histories.* Public Health Monograph No. 77. Washington, D.C.: U.S. Government Printing Office, 1968.

two groups appear at both ends of the distribution of number of residences. Few respondents were born in Alaska (those reporting only one residence), and of those born outside the state, a substantial number have had three or more residences prior to moving to Alaska (those reporting four or more residences in Table 3.2). This second difference is of greater significance recalling that the median age of Anchorage migrants in the sample is twenty-six. Thus, the moves made by Anchorage residents have been completed in a relatively brief period.

Another useful indicator of the propensity to migrate is the amount of time spent at a previous residence. Migration has been described as an inertial process, whereby those who remain at one location for longer periods are less likely to move (Land, 1969; Morrison, 1967). Thirty-six percent of the Anchorage migrants had lived in another community less than five years before moving to Alaska; roughly 10 percent had lived there five to nine years; and an additional 23 percent had spent between ten and nineteen years at their last residence. The remainder (31 percent) had been living at least twenty years in their former communities. Because the distribution falls largely into the first and last temporal categories, it would appear that there are two distinct groups, representing different patterns of migration, moving to Alaska. However, because most people move to the state while in their mid- to late twenties (regardless of whether they moved recently or long ago), the composition of these groups is probably similar. Both are likely to have completed some level of formal education and to have started working before moving to Alaska, the difference in numbers of years spent at a previous residence attributable to choice of school or job (near or distant from the region in which one was reared).

From what places do migrants to Anchorage come? As one might expect, they have traditionally migrated from the western United States, particularly the Pacific Northwest. More than half of the sample have lived in one of the Pacific states at some point in their lives, and over one-third moved to Alaska directly from that region (Table 3.3). This corresponds to research concerning the effects of distance on migration, in which demographers have found that migration decreases as the distance between place of origin and place of destination increases (Shaw, 1975). As mentioned, one reason for this outcome is the high costs associated with distant moves. Another explanation suggests that as the distance between migrant origin and destination increases, the amount of information concerning the destination available to migrants decreases.[5]

5. These explanations are paralleled by evidence that nineteenth-century pioneers moved westward from adjacent regions, not great distances from east to west (cf. Bogue, 1968; Thernstrom and Knights, 1970). Those living near the frontier were familiar with climatic and geographic characteristics of the new lands and, because of physical proximity, were better able to afford the costs of migration.

Table 3.3. Previous Residence of Migrants: Totals and Most Recent Residence Before Alaska

Region	Any Previous Residence* (Percent)	Last Residence Before Move (Percent)
Eastern U.S.	25	9
Southern U.S.	33	17
Midwestern U.S.	42	26
Rocky Mountain U.S.	17	9
Pacific U.S.	52	38
Foreign	10	2
Total	—	101† (105)

*Percentages will not total 100 percent because statistics indicate only that a respondent lived in a region at *one point* in his or her life. Consequently, these frequencies are given in percentages by number of respondents.
†Percentages do not sum to 100 percent because of rounding.

Table 3.4. Last Residence of Migrants Before Moving to Alaska by Length
of Residence in Alaska

Region	Less than 5 years (Percent)	5 to 9 years (Percent)	10 to 19 years (Percent)	20 or more years (Percent)
Eastern U.S.	5	4	17	11
Southern U.S.	21	17	17	11
Midwestern U.S.	32	17	17	39
Rocky Mountain U.S.	5	17	7	6
Pacific U.S.	32	46	42	33
Foreign	5	0	0	0
Total	100 (38)	101 (24)	100 (25)	100 (18)

To see if this pattern of regional migration persists over time, the region of last residence was crosstabulated with the respondent's length of residence in Alaska (Table 3.4). Although migration from the Pacific coast continues to supply a substantial number of newcomers to Alaska, migrants have been drawn from other regions of the country (especially the Midwest) in recent years, a likely correlate of construction and service employment related to the Alaska pipeline. The other exception is the large number of people from the Midwest who came to Alaska over twenty years ago. It is likely that many of these migrants came to the state during World War II and chose to stay.

It is useful to consider the employment histories of Anchorage residents alongside these patterns of residence. Eighty-five percent of the sample were employed when they moved to Alaska. (Those unemployed prior to moving were primarily homemakers travelling with their husbands or students recently graduated.) Almost two-thirds had held only one position prior to coming to Alaska, and fewer than one in seven had worked at three or more jobs before moving. As a group, these migrants spent an average of seven and one-half years at their last job before moving to Alaska. Most of them (84 percent) were employed in professional or managerial positions when they moved.

These statistics must be evaluated in light of the distinction between qualitatively different types of migration decisions motivated by economic factors: those moving because they have *no* job and those seeking a *better* job, defined in terms of increased salary, benefits, preferred location, and so on (Jansen, 1970). Thus, although persons may list economic reasons as crucial determinants in their decision to migrate, some appear to be "pushed" from a point of origin and others are "pulled" to a point of destination. Because most of those in the sample had jobs prior to moving, it is reasonable to conclude that the "pull" of Alaska was more important than the "push" exerted at the place of origin. Migrants to Anchorage appear to have a relatively stable employment history, choosing Alaska for its attractive qualities rather than for its appeal as a place of "last resort."

As with location of previous residence, occupation before moving to Alaska was examined over time (Table 3.5). The

Table 3.5. Previous Occupation of Migrants Outside of Alaska by Length of Residence in Alaska

Previous Occupation	Less than 5 years (Percent)	5 to 9 years (Percent)	10 to 19 years (Percent)	20 or more years (Percent)
Professional, managerial	44	38	28	29
Skilled, clerical	24	14	28	29
Unskilled	21	29	28	21
Armed services	12	19	17	21
Total	101 (34)	100 (21)	101 (18)	100 (14)

data indicate a growing number of white-collar workers and a decreasing number of military personnel coming to Alaska. The increase in professional and managerial employees moving to Alaska in recent years may be attributed to the growing influence of government and business over the control of resources in the state. This is particularly true of Anchorage, which houses the majority of state and federal employees in Alaska, as well as the corporate headquarters of the major oil companies. As with the rest of Alaska, there is a heavy dependence on the manufacture of products outside the state, and as a result, laborers have never composed the majority of the Anchorage workforce.

Marking Differences:
Alaskans Look at Themselves and Others

When these demographic ties are examined in conjunction with the economic and political linkages of Alaska to the United States, it becomes clear that one cannot understand daily life in Anchorage without considering the position of Alaska within a larger national system. This locational element cannot be overstated, for the fundamental similarities that bind Anchorage residents to other Americans greatly overshadow their differences. No one is more aware of this fact than the residents of Anchorage themselves. In moving to Alaska, few envision rejecting a way of life they have become accustomed to elsewhere. One indication of this emerged when I questioned Anchorage migrants about their decisions to move. When asked why they had come to Alaska, they selected "to live a pioneer's life, to be self-reliant" as eighth out of a possible ten choices. As a reason for *staying* in the state, the same response appeared as eleventh out of fourteen. On the whole, residents of Anchorage rely on supermarkets for what they eat, construction contractors for where they live, and automobile manufacturers for where they travel.

But even if conditions required a greater demonstration of self-reliance on the part of local residents, it is doubtful whether they would welcome the opportunity to live without the conveniences of modern life. A 1979 survey of Alaskan residents conducted by the State Division of Lands Management revealed that about half of those interested in homesteading desired adequate television reception immediately after moving to bush Alaska. When asked which services they would like to have within ten years of moving, they chose shopping malls third (after grocery stores and elementary schools).

In portraying Anchorage residents in this manner, it is easy to conclude that they are no different from others who live in American communities of comparable size. To some extent, such a conclusion is warranted: to them, everyday life in bush Alaska seems as distasteful as it would to most Americans comfortable in a world of urban amenities. But to phrase this comparison in such gross terms is to misrepresent the form a "frontier lifestyle" has assumed in the twentieth century. The role of the contemporary American pioneer is to be found somewhere in between the streets of downtown Seattle and the untamed wilderness of the Alaskan bush. As one resident put it, the people of Anchorage might well be called "pseudo-pioneers," those "half-way" between persons who had never come to Alaska and those seeking a subsistence lifestyle in the rougher corners of the Alaskan landscape. A young man who worked for an oil company and lived in suburban Anchorage spoke for many of his neighbors:

> I enjoy living in Alaska because it affords my kids the opportunity to be raised in a good environment. They can enjoy what I call the "wilderness experience," a sort of short-term self-reliance. I have no desire to live in a log cabin. (male, 35, biologist, three years in Alaska)

It is this half-way status that sets urban Alaskans apart from other Americans, and this difference figures prominently into the way Anchorage residents view themselves and their Alaskan experiences. In describing themselves in relation to others, residents of Anchorage are not rejecting a previous way of life but instead are affirming a sense of new opportunities available in Alaska. For some, merely knowing that these opportunities exist is more important than actually exploring them:

> What do I like most about Alaska? Just the whole way of life, I guess. You feel a part of everything. . . . I don't do much differently here than I have in other states, but I feel good about the *opportunities* I have here. Even though I don't take advantage of them, they're there. The wilderness is *there,* even if I don't go to it. It makes me feel like this is *my* Alaska, mine because no other individual owns it. (male, 56, automobile parts manager, thirteen years in Alaska)

Thus, rather than deny their ties to the rest of the nation, Anchorage residents view themselves and their experiences as quintessentially American. The claims of uniqueness made by Anchorage residents are not the basis for secession; they are a plea for a focal position *within* the system of American cultural values.

A Methodological Note

Because I was interested in how Alaskans view themselves and others with regard to a number of issues, the interview schedule contained several statements drawing on various stereotypical images of Alaskans as "frontiersmen." These statements covered a range of topics, from participation in outdoor activities to beliefs regarding independence and self-reliance. Using a scale of Likert-type items (strongly agree to strongly disagree), respondents were asked their opinions of a series of statements representing four levels of response (Table 3.6). First, they were asked their opinions of the statement; second, their opinions as to how other Alaskans

Table 3.6. Replies of Respondents to Stereotypical Statements Concerning Alaskans, Mean Values for Each Level of Response, and Difference of Means Between First and Each Successive Level*

Statement	Respondent Answer for Self	Respondent Answer for Other Alaskans	Respondent Answer for Outsiders	Respondent Description of Outsiders
1. Alaskans are individuals with a great deal of resourcefulness.	4.45†	4.56	3.75‡	2.95‡
2. Alaskans are geographically mobile; they don't stay in one place for long.	3.05	3.09	3.25	3.42‡
3. Alaskans do a lot of hunting and fishing.	4.76	4.83‡	4.82	2.61‡
4. Alaskans are more concerned with making money than with job satisfaction.	3.21	3.16	4.26‡	3.44
5. Alaskans welcome adventure; they're willing to take a chance.	4.40	4.47	4.38	2.96‡

6. The natural surroundings of their environment are important to Alaskans.	4.76	4.80	3.74‡	3.81‡
7. People in Alaska don't know very much about world affairs.	1.99	1.83‡	3.87‡	2.88‡
8. When it comes to making value judgments, Alaskans rely more on their personal convictions than on the opinions of others.	4.20	4.31‡	3.74‡	3.11‡
9. Alaskans have little respect for tradition; they prefer the new to the old.	1.96	1.96	2.88‡	2.88‡
10. When it comes down to it, most Alaskans dislike government intervention.	4.71	4.75	4.29‡	4.29‡

*The sample size on which these statistics are based is 133.
†Respondents replied in terms of Likert-type items, in which a score of 5 equalled "strongly agree" and a score of 1 equalled "strongly disagree." Thus, higher mean scores indicate greater agreement with the statement.
‡Significant at $p < 0.05$.

would respond to the statement; and third, their opinions as to how Outsiders (non-residents) would respond to the statement. A fourth question concerned the degree to which the statement was true of other Americans not living in Alaska. Using the first statement as an illustration, we have the following series of questions:

Alaskans are individuals with a great deal of resourcefulness.

1. How do you feel about this statement? (Respondent)

2. How do you think others living in Alaska would respond to this statement? (Other Alaskans)

3. How do you think those living outside of Alaska would respond to this statement? (Outsiders)

4. Finally, do you agree or disagree with this statement as it applies to most Americans living outside of Alaska? That is, are *most Americans* individuals with a great deal of resourcefulness? (Description of Outsiders)

This method allows for a comparison between the opinions of Anchorage residents and those they believe are held by others.[6] From previous research regarding group identity, we would expect Anchorage residents to believe that other Alaskans hold the same opinions as themselves and that they view both the behavior and opinions of non-residents as contrasting markedly with their opinions of Alaskans. The remainder of this section discusses these two hypotheses in greater detail.

6. This requires conducting a difference of means test between respondents' opinions of Alaskans and those they believe to be held by other groups. This methodological approach is similar to that used by Biddle et al. (1966:302–310).

Alaskans on Alaska

The data summarized in column 1 of Table 3.6 suggest that Anchorage residents share the belief that Alaskans exemplify many of the favorable traits traditionally associated with earlier American pioneers. They see themselves and their neighbors as resourceful and adventurous individuals capable of forming their own opinions on important issues. They express an appreciation of their environment and spend a large portion of their leisure time fishing and hunting in the less populated regions of the state. They are opposed to government regulation of Alaskan lands, as well as other aspects of federal and state control. Of equal importance is what those interviewed feel they are *not:* perpetual wanderers who have come to Alaska to make a "fast buck," provincialists who are ignorant of events elsewhere, or crass modernists who are insensitive to established ways and customs. Overall, the results are not surprising: Anchorage residents chose to highlight the desirable and downplay the undesirable qualities of Alaskans. The remarks of these Anchorage residents serve to illustrate:

Alaskans are down-to-earth people. They're not hung up on riches or a "Newport beach" type of life. (male, 28, real estate agent, lifetime resident of Alaska)

How would I describe Alaskans? They're a different breed altogether. They're friendly, yet independent. (male, 49, unemployed, eleven years in Alaska)

A different kind of person lives here. There is less of a structured lifestyle in Alaska, not as much of a desire to conform and more room for individual personalities. People feel more responsibility about taking care of their neighbors. (female, 32, secretary, five years in Alaska)

We're independent to be what we want to be in Alaska. We can't be comfortable Outside now. There's no big rat race. There are no social peer pressures which dictate how to live your life according to your income. (male, 46, salesman, six years in Alaska)

It is interesting to note the similarities between the opinions held by respondents themselves and those they attribute to other Alaskans. On all but three statements, there is no statistically significant difference between the two responses (comparing the first two columns of Table 3.6). In those three instances in which differences occur, however, respondents reported that other Alaskans shared the same opinions as themselves but to a greater degree. Thus, those interviewed appeared to err on the side of caution to the extent that they believe other state residents feel even more strongly about the outdoor orientation, knowledge of current events, and independent decisionmaking qualities of Alaskans.

It is possible to view the emphasis that Anchorage residents place on the frontier aspects of Alaska in terms of characterizations of the state as a land of economic opportunity. In his reformulation of the Turner thesis, Lerner (1957) suggested that the qualities associated with American pioneers evolved out of both contact with the land and life in the marketplace. As a result of this overlap between sources of frontier imagery, economic opportunists of the nineteenth century were able to capitalize on the unique aspects of western regions in support of resource development and exploitation. In this sense, the West was hardly a frontier at all, but instead an ideological justification for the same type of urban industrialism that had occurred in the eastern regions of the nation:

[The frontier myth enabled city dwellers] to live in a very unfrontier-like way and still regard themselves as frontiersmen, to develop massive corporate organizations while speaking of the individual entrepreneur, and to build up a Big Government with a far-flung imperium while still cherishing in politics the cult of the log cabin and the whistle-stop, back-platform campaign speech. (Lerner, 1957:168)

The seemingly limitless potentialities of Alaska support the belief that those who have chosen to live in the state are a select group of Americans. Over a third of the people interviewed reported that economic opportunity was one of the things they liked most about living in Alaska.

Alaska is the only state in the Union where you can get an idea one week and see it grow [the next]. You can do a lot of things here. (male, 50, executive officer in Native foundation, lifetime resident of Alaska)

Alaska affords you the opportunity to go farther faster in your profession. You can do as much as you can do and be as good as you can be here. (female, 33, health planner, three years in Alaska)

Alaska provides the economic opportunity to do what you want. It's easier to start a business here, to make a name for yourself. (male, 29, accountant, four years in Alaska)

I feel like an Alaskan because there's the sense that, up here, you're building something. Everything's not already done. (male, 27, drilling supervisor, two years in Alaska)

This emphasis on the opportunities available to Alaskans is particularly salient among women living in Anchorage. Their comments suggest that sexual stratification is less prevalent in Alaska than in other areas of the country and that women can participate in spheres of activity, primarily economic and political, to which they might be denied access elsewhere. The remarks of two women living in Anchorage serve to illustrate:

People don't have prejudiced attitudes here. There is less sex discrimination. People don't measure you by your income or by where you live. There's less stratification. (female, 25, air traffic controller, six years in Alaska)

The economic opportunity here is good. If something happened to my husband, I could always make a living here. I couldn't do that Outside. I think women are treated more equally here. I've been able to run our business in Alaska, and I might not have tried this had we stayed Outside. (female, 40, general contractor, fourteen years in Alaska)

All of these comments are framed in terms of a comparison with previous experiences outside of Alaska. In each case, life in Alaska is thought to be better than that seen in other parts of the country. As the following section documents, this elevated status of the landscape of Alaska has been transferred to the residents and to their neighbors.

On the Inside Looking Out

One of the first things a newcomer to Alaska notices is that virtually all Alaskans refer to non-residents as Outsiders.[7] This label, which boasts connotations of state chauvinism, is a part of everyday conversation, a continual reminder that other Americans know very little about Alaska or its inhabitants. When asked about the opinions Outsiders have of Alaskans (level three responses in the line of questioning), about half (51 percent) of those I interviewed felt that non-residents would have no basis for judgment in at least one of the ten statements.[8] Comments such as "They have no way of knowing what we're like" were common, as residents were quick to stress the importance of having lived

7. Groups frequently assign a label to non-members to define their boundaries. For a discussion of how this functions to strengthen group cohesion, see Kanter (1972:169–175).

8. The statements that received the highest percentage of "Outsiders don't know" responses were "Alaskans are geographically mobile; they don't stay in one place for long" (25 percent); "Alaskans are individuals with a great deal of resourcefulness" (24 percent); and "When it comes to making value judgments, Alaskans rely more on their personal opinions than on the opinions of others" (18 percent).

in Alaska as a necessary precondition to forming opinions about Alaskans. Those who voiced a concern over Outsider ignorance shared the belief that meaningful description of Alaska rested on insider information and experience.

Although a lack of information on the part of non-residents was a source of concern for many Anchorage residents, their major reservations lay in the belief that Outsiders possess inaccurate information about Alaska. In seven out of the ten statements in Table 3.6, the opinions residents held of Alaskans differed significantly from those they believed to be held by non-residents (a comparison of columns 1 and 3). As one might expect, residents feel that Outsiders systematically underrate the favorable qualities and overestimate the unfavorable qualities of Alaskans. In their opinions, non-residents emphasize the self-centered side of Alaskans—their concern for big salaries, disinterest in world affairs, and apparent lack of respect for tradition—while at the same time belittle the admirable traits of state residents, such as their resourcefulness and environmental orientation.

It would appear that Alaskans' beliefs regarding Outside information about their state are more than mere conjecture. In a 1981 survey, residents of the continental United States were asked a number of questions about Alaska, ranging from the physical and social characteristics of Alaska and Alaskans to views concerning Alaskan resources and revenues (Dittman Research Corporation, 1981). Their responses not only indicate a lack of information about the state, but also reveal a naivéte concerning several of the gross physical characteristics of Alaska. For example, in answer to the question, "What is the relationship between Alaska and the continental United States?," only 85 percent responded that Alaska was a state. Five percent thought it was a separate country; 4 and 2 percent believed Alaska to be a territory or a commonwealth, respectively; and 4 percent did not know the political status of Alaska. Over 60 percent thought that at least half of Alaska was covered by snow, glaciers, and ice most of the year. (The area that meets this description is approximately 5 percent of the total area of the state.) As a group, respondents grossly overestimated the population of Alaska. Over one-third of the sample believed the state contained in excess of a million residents; the 1980 census, by contrast, recorded a total state population of less than half that number. The population itself was thought to be largely composed of Alaskan Natives. About two-thirds of the respondents believed that half or more of Alaska's population consisted of Natives. The actual number is closer to 16 percent.

In many respects these descriptions of Alaska come as no surprise. Only 7 percent of those responding to the 1981 survey had ever been in Alaska. For the most part, they know only the image of Alaska as portrayed through the media. Nearly 60 percent of those surveyed obtained their information about Alaska from newspapers, television, or periodicals; less than 10 percent had ever spoken with a visitor to the state. Given the substantial expense of travelling to Alaska, such limited contact with the state is to be expected.[9]

Two consequences result from what Anchorage residents believe to be ignorance or inaccurate description on the part of Outsiders. The first reflects a concern that Outside opinion does not realistically portray the economic and political conditions of the state. Because the history of Alaska has been shaped largely in accordance with federal policy, state residents continue to view long-distance advice as undesirable meddling.[10] Alaskans believe that repeated efforts by the federal government to deal with the state as a territorial possession cloud the contemporary realities of life in the forty-ninth state and tend to further distinguish them from people who do not live in Alaska. As one resident put

9. Similar findings regarding sources of information and descriptions of Alaska are apparent among migrants to Alaska. See Chapter 5.

10. When asked what they disliked most about living in Alaska, the fourth most frequent response (mentioned by 16 percent of those interviewed) was the extent of federal control in Alaska.

it, "The rest of the United States does not treat us like a state." Others offered similar descriptions:

> Alaska is not a state; it's a political football. Government employees are toys that people in D.C. like to play with. (male, 39, salesman, two years in Alaska)

> There is a lack of understanding that Alaska is a state. We have an inability to get services which are given to all the other states. We're isolated. Washington decisions are founded in an Eastern mentality. They see us as a colony, and don't take into account the values of the people living here. Part of it is the five-hour time difference between us. That serves to cut off communication. But if we all left, what's Uncle Sam going to do then? Roll in the first brigade? They don't appreciate what we go through up here. (male, 35, systems analyst, one year in Alaska)

Here again, the opinions of Outsiders responding to the Alaska national survey are telling. Non-residents express a continued preference for a large measure of external control over Alaskan affairs. When asked which level of government they felt was most qualified to run the affairs of Alaska, over 40 percent mentioned the federal government. Throughout a series of questions dealing with Alaskan resources and revenues, respondents asserted that the state's resources could be developed without serious harm to the environment. Furthermore, a substantial number believe that funds derived from resource development in Alaska should be shared with other states (Dittman Research Corporation, 1981). This extension of colonial status beyond statehood is what provokes anger among residents of Alaska. In the face of what Outsiders view as the site of great wealth, Alaskans point to the substandard public services that plague many local communities. In doing so, they again draw attention to the importance of insider status in laying claim to knowing anything about Alaska.

The second consequence of a lack of accurate information concerning contemporary Alaska is the perpetuation of a feeling of singularity among Anchorage residents. In light of the limited contact most Americans have with Alaska, Outsiders are often fascinated with the frontier lifestyle assumed to be characteristic of residents of the forty-ninth state. Over half of those interviewed in the Alaska national survey stated that people who choose to live in Alaska possessed different attitudes and characteristics from those living in the rest of the United States. In my own survey data, there were many indications that when Anchorage residents return to the continental United States to visit family or friends, they encounter such evidence of their distinctiveness directly:

> Outsiders think we're taking a chance just by living here. (female, 18, homemaker, lifetime resident of Alaska)

> When we visit Outside, my friends still ask me questions like "Where do you shop for groceries that is like a Safeway store?" (male, 55, business advisor, nine years in Alaska)

> Outsiders think that we still live in igloos. (male, 62, retired, thirty years in Alaska)

> Outsiders think of us as self-reliant. They try to put us with the people of the Old West. You know, a "stare 'em in the eye" image. (male, 25, automobile mechanic, three years in Alaska)

> I really felt like an Alaskan when, after a couple of years up here, I returned to California for a visit. Everyone had dreamy visions and their eyes lit up when I told them I was from Alaska. (male, 32, dentist, four years in Alaska)

It is not surprising, then, to find that one of the reasons Anchorage residents come to see themselves as unique is because others treat them that way. Several of those interviewed (18 percent) noted that they began to think of themselves as Alaskans only after they had travelled outside of the state. Because the isolation and distant location of Alaska limit the interactions between residents and non-residents of the state, the perceived differences between the two groups are highlighted when they come into contact with one another.

It follows from this analysis that residents of Anchorage have carved out a unique and decidedly more favorable place for themselves amid the larger American population. In all but one of the ten stereotype statements (Table 3.6, comparing columns 1 and 4), they described themselves in terms significantly different from Outsiders. Even more important than the number of differences residents noted between themselves and others is the ubiquity associated with their responses, as none of the social characteristics thought to influence attitudes—age, sex, education, occupation, income—exerts a significant effect on these description of Alaskans.[11] The belief that Alaskans were different from other Americans often appeared as a foregone conclusion among Anchorage residents. Alaskans were unique simply because they had moved to—and stayed—in Alaska. Two residents summed up these differences succinctly:

People in the Lower 48 can't deal with the extremes we have to [deal with] here. (male, 28, mechanic, two years in Alaska)

If most people welcomed adventure, they'd be here. (male, 46, salesman, six years in Alaska)

Testing the Bonds of Commonality

The sentiments expressed by Alaskans toward other Americans often appear to be vague and without direction. In fact, it is only when they are centered on a particular issue that they are brought into sharper focus. This was evident

11. This conclusion is based on a number of tests of association that failed to demonstrate a significant effect ($p < 0.05$) of any group trait.

in the comments of the residents cited previously who began to identify with Alaska only after interacting with non-Alaskans. Occasions such as visiting friends and family and vacationing "Outside" serve as moments for reflection on one's identity and sense of place. They are a subset of a general class of events in which our sense of attachments is called into question, times when we must demonstrate to ourselves, as well as to others, the fundamental characteristics that unite or divide us. Opportunities for this type of differentiation may be fortuitous (as when a middle class suburban homemaker is forced to share an elevator with a bag lady), or they may be purposely staged (as when a diplomatic conference is held). In the latter case, we might think of a person or group as creating opportunities for displays of their differences.

Opportunities thus created may highlight group differences in two ways. In some instances, an interchange between two groups may be premised on the notion that there is little that both share. When these two groups occupy the same society or culture, the most extreme form such a display could take would be a declaration of secession. As Shils (1975:59) notes:

> An act of secession is the most pronounced form of collective refusal to continue membership in a society. It is the result of a decision not to live under the political authority of that society, but it is more than that. . . . Secession would create an ostensibly new and separate, distinctive society, although it would not necessarily change the internal order of the new society very much from what it was when it was a subordinate part of the society in which it was hitherto included.

Secessionist attempts have in common their emphasis upon territorial, institutional, and nominal separateness and to that end are paralleled by utopian experiments (Kanter, 1972). Such a radical severance of ties is illustrated in the Mormon migration of 1846. The essential feature that distinguished the Mormons from other pioneers of that time was their break, both ideologically and economically, with the rest of the nation. They were looking for a new life independent of the criticisms of others. They had not left a home in Illinois, for in many ways the Mormons were coming, rather than leaving, home when they reached Salt Lake. In a very real sense, the Mormons had been driven out of the United States, not merely to its edge. Because they refused to look eastward, the standards they set were their own. They were at the center of a new world, not at the edges of an old one.

Brigham Young realized the importance of economic self-sufficiency to this cause. His message to the early settlers was clear:

> We do not intend to have any trade or commerce with the gentile world, for so long as we buy of them we are in a degree dependent upon them. The Kingdom of God cannot rise independent of the gentile nations until we produce, manufacture and make every article of use, convenience, or necessity among our own people. I am determined to cut every thread of this kind and live free and independent, untrammeled by any of their detestable customs and practices. (quoted in Arrington and Bitton, 1979:122)

To establish Salt Lake City as a community dependent on eastern manufacturing would have defeated the purpose of the Mormon migration. Dependence would also have meant that the way of life sought by the Mormons was perhaps not that different from the one they left behind.

The Mormon experience and others like it share an emphasis on the curtailment of relations between two groups. On the basis of the conclusion that differences make "peaceful" interaction impossible, separation appears as the sole alternative.

In many other situations, however, the process of differentiation serves yet another purpose, that of allowing groups that share fundamental similarities to identify themselves as distinct from one another. Here, terminating relations between groups is not something sought after; rather, it is something to be avoided. David Riesman (1954) has described this process as one of "marginal differentiation," whereby groups seek to appear different from one another *but not too different.* The dilemma thus engendered is one of negotiating a path between social conformity (which implies little or no differentiation) and social deviance (which implies an excessive measure of differentiation).

This is the central question with which members of the Alaska Statehood Commission struggled for over two years. On August 26, 1980, Alaskan voters went to the polls to vote on the question: "Shall the Alaska Statehood Commission be convened to study the status of the people of Alaska within the United States and to consider and recommend appropriate changes in the relationship of Alaska to the United States?" A slight majority of them answered yes, and two months later in Fairbanks, the Statehood Commission started to work.

As the commissioners later noted, this was the first time since the Civil War that the residents of any state had formally requested a critical assessment of statehood. This comparison to the secessionist efforts of the Confederacy grossly distorts the nature of the work of the Statehood Commission, although it no doubt influenced the vote on the referendum question. Various local groups within Alaska, such as Alaskans for Independence, touted the ballot issue as a chance for residents to "correct the mistake" made in opting for statehood in 1958. The commission spent its first several months trying to dispel these connotations of secession, but even after its final report had been distributed, the sensationalism of political separatism remained. This was nowhere evident than in the brief national coverage that accompanied the retiring of the Statehood Commission. The headline for the Associated Press story reporting this event read "Alaskans Decide Not to Secede."

In its twenty-seven months of operation the Alaska Statehood Commission held meetings throughout the state to discuss its charge and to solicit public comment. It contracted fourteen studies totalling over 2,000 pages, ranging from an oral history of Alaskan statehood to an analysis of the flow of revenues between the state and federal governments. Three areas of investigation occupied the majority of the commission's attention: progress made on implementation of the Alaska Statehood Act; comparative experiences of other states and American possessions in relation to the federal government; and alternative forms of association possible between Alaska and the United States (e.g., commonwealth status, free association, territoriality, partition, legal independence).

The history of the Alaska Statehood Commission, however, is not one of constant debate over the benefits and liabilities of secession. Rather, it dramatically illustrates the process of marginal differentiation along a variety of dimensions—economic, political, and demographic. In reviewing the role of Alaska within the United States, the commission employed a strategy whereby both similarities and differences between Alaska and other states were addressed. This comparative approach was used not only to identify the problems of Alaska within the federal system, but also to construct a response to these problems. The process of differentiation assumed the following sequence:

First, the numerous similarities of Alaska to other states were underscored. The case was made that the ties that bind Alaskans to other Americans were stronger than their differences. Nowhere was this more evident than in the Statehood Commission's dismissal of independence as an alternative status for Alaska. After discarding arguments regarding the numerous legal, economic, and military prohibitions associated with independence, the commission outlined what it described as "the real case against independence":

> The overwhelming majority of Alaskans, including all members of this commission, consider themselves Americans. . . . We are proud to be citizens of a nation which responded so generously [to the devastation wrought by the Good Friday earthquake], and want to

pass on this citizenship to our descendants. That citizenship bestows the right to travel freely in the rest of the states, states from which many of us hail, where relations live and ancestors lie buried. . . . These bonds cannot be severed at a whim. . . . In short, vast reserves of loyalty stand between Alaska and independence. (Alaska Statehood Commission, 1982:40)

As noted earlier in this chapter, the deepest ties between Alaska and the rest of the nation stem from the migrant status of its population. Here, that status was expressed in terms of political self-denomination, and American citizenship was thought to provide the context for all discussions of the role of Alaska *within* the federal system.

Second, premised on these similarities, Alaskan issues and problems were aligned with those of other states. As a result, pressing local concerns were presented as part of larger national problems. Thus, for example, complaints regarding the large federal presence in Alaska were couched in terms of "a nation of federal dependence." Citing a number of studies by the Advisory Commission on Intergovernmental Relations, the Statehood Commission concluded that "most units of government in the United States have, in 20 years, been transformed from being mostly independent of federal benefaction into being beggars that compete for it" (Alaska Statehood Commission, 1982:27).

In those instances in which the problem was not shared by all states, comparisons were drawn to a subset of the nation. This strategy was most notably illustrated in references to the substantial federal land holdings in western states. Although the commission did not recommend that Alaska join the legal battles fought by proponents of the "Sagebrush Rebellion" (a political movement in several western states to gain control of federally-owned land), it emphatically stresses that "the western resource states are our natural allies in other important matters" (Alaska Statehood Commission, 1982:23). Similar parallels were noted between Alaska and other non-contiguous sections of the United

States—Hawaii and the unincorporated territories. Here, investigations by the Statehood Commission revealed that "Alaska and the noncontiguous possessions share problems with transportation and other laws that may discriminate against them or that fail to apply logically to states and possessions separated from the rest of the country" (Alaska Statehood Commission, 1982:26).

Third, problems that had been portrayed as general to the nation were described as having reached dramatic proportions in Alaska. Alaska was singled out as the battleground where the principal issues surrounding federal-state relations had crystallized. The commission's opening remarks put the case bluntly:

> The federal presence is greater in Alaska than in any other state. Because Alaska is strategically located next to the Soviet Union and commands polar air routes, there is a heavy—and largely welcome—national military presence. By being non-contiguous, Alaska also feels the negative impact of law designed for commerce between contiguous states. Having international borders, Alaska finds itself the object of treaty-making. . . . With 74 percent of the nation's potentially oil-rich Outer Continental Shelf surrounding Alaska, the federal government says that the wishes of the state to cushion fisheries and coastal towns from the impacts of drilling must give way in the national interest to the goal of energy self-sufficiency. (Alaskan Statehood Commission, 1982:1)

Thus, the various qualities that the state shares with other parts of the national system assume a unique configuration in Alaska. Although it is obvious that other states and possessions are non-contiguous, that other states are rich in natural resources, and that other areas of the country are vital to national security, Alaska was represented as the *intersection* of these (and yet other) particulars. The principal irony of this display of marginal differentiation, then, was the way in which an accumulation of similarities became the basis for marking differences.

Fourth, because Alaska occupies a unique place in the drama of federal-state relations, it was concluded that the state should assume a position of leadership in the struggle to regain local autonomy; Alaska should occupy a leadership role in the formation of coalitions that would unite the states and possessions with which it shares some quality. The final report of the Statehood Commission begins with such a declaration:

> History, economics and technology have combined to offer Alaska a chance for leadership beyond its borders. Once isolated, but no more, Alaska must become a vigorous actor on the national scene, eager to dispel ignorance about itself, a state eager to support the powers of all states, a state willing to break new trails with others states in forming new compacts and coalitions to solve mutual problems. Alaska must speak out against abuses of federal power, in the press and in the courts and in councils of the states and of the nation. (Alaska Statehood Commission, 1983:2)

This challenging response embodies the essential duality of a marginal status. Alaska is held out as "the source of America's future" (as one Statehood commissioner remarked), while at the same time, the point is made that effective leadership must attract a following. The unique position of Alaska within the federal system is not taken to mean that it is any "less American" than other states. Rather, the opposite case is made: Alaska is the embodiment of the American character.

This illustration of how Alaskans define their place in the nation draws attention to the locations most likely to engage in marginal differentiation. Some places within a social system may be more conducive to the processes of marking differences than others. More specifically, the tensions that accompany marginal differentiation are strongest near the edges of a system. Because Alaska is both distant and non-contiguous from the remainder of the country, its place within the national system is tenuous. The benefits to participation in that system, then, appear weak or are likely to be obscured, a feeling so clearly expressed by the Anchorage residents I interviewed. And although it is not surprising to find that Alaskans created a public forum for discussion of their ties to the nation, it is likewise to be expected that the outcome of such an endeavor was to reaffirm strongly their link to other Americans.

Put simply, without their connection to the rest of the nation, Alaskans would lose their role of defining the edge—the frontier—of the country. It is in opposition to the center of the nation that the frontier status of Alaska is created.

As part of a general process, the case of Alaska points to the critical role that others play in acquiring the self. No place is devoid of the raw materials that kindle such a comparison of the self with others.[12] With customary eloquence, Erving Goffman (1961:320) speaks to the larger issue:

> Without something to belong to, we have no stable self, and yet total commitment and attachment to any social unit implies a kind of selflessness. Our sense of being a person can come from being drawn into a wider social unit; our sense of selfhood can arise through the little ways in which we resist the pull. Our status is backed by the solid buildings of the world, while our sense of personal identity often resides in the cracks.

Just as residents of Alaska rely on other Americans to define their uniqueness, a similar process of differentiation internal to Alaska distinguishes "real Alaskans" from those who "merely reside" in the state. How newcomers to Alaska "become Alaskans" is the topic of the next chapter.

12. The structure and group identity of pastoral nomadism provide another illustration of this general process. See Khazanov (1984).

CHAPTER 4

Becoming an Alaskan

Anyone who has spent a minimal amount of time in Alaska is familiar with how residents of the state differentiate between those who merely live there and those who are "real" Alaskans. Because the state is characterized by high rates of in- and out-migration, non-residents may find it difficult to distinguish between the two groups. Nevertheless, as most migrants to Alaska soon learn, there are three identifiable stages in the process of "becoming an Alaskan": learning a regional vocabulary, adjusting to an unusual winter climate, and coping with the effects of distance from the continental United States. Together, this series of reorientations of self underscores the uniqueness of life in Alaska and fosters a comparison among groups of the Anchorage population that have lived in the state for varying amounts of time.

Of course, Anchorage is but one of a number of communities in which established residents view newcomers as different from themselves. And for that reason, it is helpful to begin this discussion of becoming an Alaskan with a few general remarks concerning the experiences that accompany migration.

Acquiring a Sense of Place

Although the symbolic dimension of community is deeply rooted in the discipline of sociology, few sociologists have

Chapter 4 was published in slightly different form as "Reorientations of Self: Residential Identification in Anchorage, Alaska," in *Studies in Symbolic Interaction* 5 (1984): 219–237. It appears here courtesy of JAI Press, Inc.

been directly concerned with the process through which residents come to identify with a specific place. Newcomers to any community encounter a number of practical difficulties that accompany relocation, but post-migration adjustment involves a great deal more than reorientation to a new physical environment. At the same time that new arrivals confront a physical world devoid of familiarities, they also enter a symbolic world of established traditions that anchor a community in social and cultural space. Just as it is naïve to suggest that physical relocation proceeds concurrently with symbolic relocation, it is equally unlikely that both processes exert equivalent influence on a newcomer's self-identity. Residential identification, through which a migrant modifies a previous definition of self to include a new symbolic world, occurs when reorientations to a new physical environment are interpreted in terms of their symbolic content.[1] When this interpretation is not forthcoming, we may observe what Maines (1978) describes as a migration of "bodies" in the absence of a migration of "selves."

This view of residential identification implies that the criteria for community membership are derived from and, in turn, sustain the symbolic culture of a community. On their way to "becoming" community members, newcomers encounter pre-existing standards for membership, and to the extent that new arrivals incorporate these standards into their own identities, they reinforce the collective sentiments of the community. This characterization directs attention to the interactive nature of residential identification: identification with a community is not solely a matter of individual action but is, in large measure, a product of the actions of others. Maines (1978:246) addresses this concern when he writes: "Identity, or the person's meaning, is always

1. The sense in which I am using the term *residential identification* is similar to Bardo and Bardo's (1980:202) definition of *commitment:* "The elaboration of new identities, the reformulation of old identities, and the individual's integration in the new social milieux through the development of side bets."

negotiated to some degree through others' acts of placing us in some social category as well as our announcing to others those categories in which we see ourselves or in which we wish to be placed."

Because residential identification is a negotiated outcome of the interactions of newcomers and others, established residents may dispute the claims to community membership made by new arrivals. These two groups not only may disagree as to the time when identification has been achieved, but also may differ in their interpretation of the criteria for identification themselves. Similarly, one would expect differences in standards imposed for community membership to affect the frequency and level of residential identification. In some places, identification with a community may be impeded by standards of membership that prescribe characteristics of ascription that newcomers may not possess. In others, community membership may be readily accessible to those who possess specified characteristics of achievement.

A number of ascribed characteristics may influence a newcomer's identification with a place, as well as his or her acceptance by others into a new community. Blacks who move into white neighborhoods or non-Italians who enter Italian neighborhoods may find it difficult to feel a part of the community. Men may be denied admission to an exclusively female college, and male exchange students at such a place may fail to identify—or be identified by others—with the college community. Because of their demographic composition, areas that harbor large numbers of retirees may be avoided by young people seeking to relocate. Even in places characterized by heterogeneity of race, ethnicity, sex, or age, other ascribed traits, such as birth in the community, may be requisite for residential identification. Newcomers to a small town with relatively little in- and out-migration may find that established residents reserve community membership for those sharing a common birthright.

Rather than inhibit the formation of residential identity among those who do not share certain ascribed traits, areas that witness rapid population turnover may provide ready access to avenues of community identification. In response to the recent influx of population into south Texas, for example, Rice University began a series of non-credit courses for newcomers to Houston "who want to bridge cultural shock and learn to walk, talk and eat like a Texan" (Cohen, 1979). Far from placing identification as an "urban cowboy" outside the reach of new arrivals, this program, entitled "Living Texas," suggests that classroom participation is one convenient way of "becoming a Texan." And because Houston is largely populated by newcomers to the state, those who enroll in "Living Texas" classes may indeed begin to feel more like Texans than others who have arrived recently.

Although this illustration perhaps characterizes residential identification in a superficial manner, it nevertheless exemplifies the various ways through which migrants achieve a sense of place in new surroundings. In Anchorage, residential identification also entails a process of achievement whereby migrants pass through a series of reorientations on their way to becoming Alaskans. In the process of achieving the "Alaskan" label, newcomers to Anchorage master a new language by acquiring a frontier vocabulary, cope with the pronounced effects of distance from the continental United States, and manage a disorienting sense of time that follows from seasonal fluctuations in the length of daylight hours. Together, these reorientations of language, space, and time form the basis of community identification for Anchorage residents and contribute to the construction and maintenance of a symbolic culture in Anchorage. The process of becoming an Alaskan affects daily life in Anchorage in three distinct ways.

First, these reorientations form necessary (but not sufficient) conditions for staying in Alaska. Residents of Anchorage who fail to routinize procedures for coping with the effects of isolation and darkness are more likely to leave the state than those who arrive at stable solutions to these difficulties. In this sense, the process of becoming an Alaskan must progress, as Shibutani puts it, from "adaptation" to "adjustment."[2]

Second, these reorientations provide the basis for differentiation among groups of the Anchorage population that have lived in the state for varying amounts of time. Because identification as an Alaskan involves a process of achievement in which newcomers adopt the standards established by previous residents, Anchorage residents make different—and at times disputed—claims to group membership.

Third, in interpreting these reorientations as components of a frontier experience, residents of Anchorage emphasize the unique qualities of Alaskan life. Residents assert that persons living in other communities of the country do not experience similar hardships and then employ this claim to bolster their symbolic construction of Alaska as the final American frontier.

A Frontier Vocabulary: Reorientation of Language

One of the fundamental institutions that facilitates group identification is language. A newcomer to a group finds that members share a previously circumscribed universe of discourse and may or may not realize that understanding the ways of the group requires mastering a new language. In acquiring the language of the group, new arrivals not only come to view themselves as group members, but also become participants in the "symbolic environment" of the group (Shibutani, 1961:490). Adoption of a common dialect, then, implies identification with the group's history and a shared perception of the group's location in social and cultural space. As Mills (1939:677) writes: "Along with language, we acquire a set of social norms and values. A vocabulary is

---

2. "In contrast with the concept of adjustment, which refers to an organism's coming to terms with the exigencies of specific situations, adaptation refers to the more stable solutions—well organized ways of coping with typical problems which become crystallized through a succession of adjustments." (Shibutani, 1961:87)

not merely a string of words; immanent within it are societal textures—institutional and political coordinates. Back of every vocabulary lie sets of collective action."

Residents of Anchorage, like those living in other regions of the country, employ a vernacular unique to their surroundings, and learning to "talk like an Alaskan" is the first step in becoming an Alaskan. The evaluative statements implicit in the regional vocabulary of Anchorage residents express three themes: a distinction between those living in Alaska and those living in other areas of the country; a distinction among groups of state residents; and an identification with the state as a whole, rather than with Anchorage itself—a distinction that emphasizes the more primitive side of Alaskan life.

As noted in the previous chapter, newcomers to Alaska frequently hear Alaskans describe non-residents as "Outsiders" and any place that is not Alaska as "Outside."[3] (Some substitute "Lower 48" for "Outside," and old-timers might still say "Stateside.") Failure to adopt these familiar references to the people and places left behind is an immediate signal to established residents that they are speaking to a newcomer.

In a similar manner, language becomes a vehicle for marking differences between those who merely reside in the state and those who are "real Alaskans." The former are called "Cheechakos" and the latter "Sourdoughs," both linguistic vestiges from the days of the Alaska gold rush. *Cheechako* is a derivative of *Chicago* and refers to the inexperience displayed by newcomers to Alaska. A Sourdough, on the other hand, was a veteran prospector, the name coming from the bread carried on the trail. Because these two terms connote achieved status differences, the words of old-timers are sometimes used to legitimate the claims of individuals or organizations. In a frequently aired

3. Groups and cultures frequently assign non-members a label to define their boundaries. For a discussion of how this functions to strengthen group ties, see Kanter (1972:169–175).

television announcement, the oil companies insisted that what's good for them is what's good for the people of Alaska:

Narrator: It's a pressure job, drilling for oil and gas in Alaska. Bad weather, hard-to-get-to locations, and high exploratory costs.

Sourdough: Any real Alaskan wants these explorations to go on. For Pete's sake, it's the only way our economy is going to grow.

Of major importance is the fact that local residents never refer to themselves as "Anchoragites." For those who have seen the urban sprawl of Alaska's largest city, this observation comes as little surprise. Alternately portrayed as the "American nightmare" by Norman Mailer and as an "instant Albuquerque" by John McPhee, Anchorage appears as anything but a frontier settlement. Nevertheless, despite the presence of glass office buildings, paved streets, and residential suburbs, the livelier aspects of Alaska's past live on in the daily conversations of Anchorage residents.

Many of these characterizations have their origin in times when climate played a major role in affecting the course of Alaskan life. The restless, claustrophobic feeling that accompanies the long hours of winter darkness is familiarly known as cabin fever. Placing bets on the dates of "freeze up" and "break up" is an annual event, as is speculation over when the "termination dust" (first snow of the season) will arrive. "White out" is not an office supply but a hazardous condition caused by ice fog, in which light reflects off the snow casting no shadow. A cache used to be a place where food was stored out of the reach of wild animals; today, it usually refers to a business and is often preceded by an appropriate product name (e.g., The Book Cache, The Stamp and Coin Cache). (One bank has named its overnight teller machine Cache 24.)

Other firms employ a northern vocabulary in describing themselves and their services. Only a partial list gleaned from a drive down the major streets of Anchorage would include Top of the World Foreign Auto Parts, Gold Streak Freight Lines, Yukon Office Supply, Arctic Blossoms (a florist), Pioneer Loan Company, Far North Taxi, Pioneer Chicken, Husky Steam Cleaners, Gold Rush Auto Sales, Frontier Transportation Company, and Grizzly Skins (a retail outlet for work clothes).[4] The frontier image of Alaska may also become part of a firm's advertising campaign. A shrewd old prospector stares out from the newspaper to remark:

> Alaska has always
> appealed to independents
> And The First National Bank
> of Anchorage
> wants to preserve that spirit

With an Independence Account, you can write as many checks as you need and pay only $2.50 per month. You are not bound by any minimum balance requirement, and you are free to take advantage of all our no-charge services.

It's part of our effort to make banking at First National as easy as possible for our busy, independent customers.

Even an apparently unlikely candidate like the Universal Life Church has appealed to the pioneer spirit of contemporary Alaskans:

Why did we come to Alaska? Why do we stay here? What are we seeking? I believe that the Alaskan dream has three ingredients: freedom, peace, and prosperity. I

---

4. Of course, businesses in other parts of the country make use of similar descriptions to emphasize regional peculiarities. For example, Massachusetts firms may employ such terms as *Pilgrim* or *Colonial* in their names and advertising. For an interesting and somewhat humorous illustration, see "Farming Connecticut Style," *New York Times,* March 29, 1981, sec. 11, p. 22. Also, Maines (1978:260) makes a similar point when he comments: "Advertising, or generically the intentional ways in which we talk about things, is another critical dimension of identity migration and proliferation."

also believe that the Universal Life Church will help you attain this dream TODAY not in some distant future. TODAY can be your day to fulfill that dream![5]

Yet out of numerous advertising appeals, the one that goes the farthest toward reshaping the frontier imagery of Alaska in contemporary fashion was launched by a company that opened a luxury hotel in Anchorage in 1979:

Announcing a New Wrinkle in Alaskan Survival:

Was a time when survival in the Great Land depended on stuffing dry grass in your mitts at −30 degrees.

But now there's a new technique in Alaskan survival—with all of the pleasures and none of the punishment.

The New Sheraton Anchorage Hotel.

If you're in town for business, the new Sheraton Anchorage is a survival station. Fifteen stories high. 410 rooms. A health club. And the largest grand ballroom in Alaska—accommodates 1,000 people.

And service has been hired for enthusiasm and trained to indulge your dreams of survival today.

Oh, don't get us wrong. We still want to you to experience the struggle, fun, and savage splendor of Alaska.

But who's to deny you a little fresh Hawaiian pineapple for breakfast and a sauna R&R before dinner?

Join our common fight for survival.

Afterall, this is Alaska.

5. Of these "three ingredients," the emphasis appears to be on prosperity, because the Universal Life Church wishes to make Alaska residents ordained ministers with tax-exempt status from the Internal Revenue Service.

Almost everywhere one looks, there are reminders that the rougher aspects of Alaska are far from dead, even in Anchorage, a community that bears little resemblance to a pioneer outpost. Whether listening to conversations among residents, walking the streets of the city, watching television, or reading the newspapers, the newcomer to Anchorage is confronted by indications that life in Alaska is different from that in other parts of the country. In making use of a frontier vocabulary, Anchorage residents continue to represent their everyday lives in a unique fashion.

Starting Over: Reorientation of Space

Coping with the effects of separation that result from residential relocation is an experience shared by all migrants as they begin to replace old familiarities with new ones. Yet because Alaska is geographically isolated from the rest of the United States, newcomers to Anchorage often feel that there are characteristics unique to their new home that make this transition more difficult than that experienced by other migrants.[6]

Depending on where they moved from, recent arrivals to Anchorage find themselves 2,000 to 5,000 miles (and as many as four time zones) west of their old homes. Most of them have driven up, so that the ten-day trip on the AlCan Highway has given them a rough idea of just how far away Alaska really is. Owing to the high costs of freight, they will have been selective in their choice of what to bring, and when they go shopping to replace what they left behind, they will find the same goods slightly more expensive, even if purchased at outlets of national retail stores. If they pick up the phone to let friends or family know that they have arrived safely, they may be annoyed by the time lag between

6. When asked what they disliked most about living in Alaska, those interviewed gave as the third most frequently mentioned response the distance of Alaska from the continental United States.

speaking and hearing that results from satellite transmission of calls. (They may also be annoyed when they receive their first telephone bill, only to discover that national long-distance rates do not apply to Alaska.) And finally, when they have at last found time to collapse in front of the television set, they may be surprised to find that programming on the national networks runs one to three weeks behind that in other parts of the country. News programs are presented via satellite delay and sports events are broadcast live, but that means that an avid Washington Redskins fan may have to rise at 7:30 on Sunday morning to catch the pre-game show.

If these seem but minor accommodations that newcomers to Anchorage must make, that is not to say that their personal sacrifices involving the loss of family and friends are more easily assuaged. Of course, migrants to Alaska are no different from others who relocate in that they desire to establish ties to new friends and acquaintances. In fact, studies of internal migration report that the desire to be near family or friends is the primary non-economic reason people give for moving in the United States (Uhlenberg, 1973; Bogue, 1977; Shaw, 1975). But because Alaska's population is largely transient (the average length of residence in Anchorage is less than ten years), Anchorage residents do not rate proximity to family and friends high on their list of reasons for moving to Alaska.[7] And because Alaska is an unlikely stop for most travellers, newcomers seldom encounter a familiar face on the streets of downtown Anchorage.

Consequently, most new arrivals to Anchorage find that the only people they know are those who came with them.[8] Despite the conveniences of modern transportation and com-

7. In the aggregate, respondents rated "to be near family or friends" as ninth out of ten factors, which might have influenced their decision to move to Alaska. See Chapter 5 for further discussion of this issue.

8. Two-thirds of the people interviewed moved to Alaska with at least one other person. (This excludes those who travelled as minors under the care of parents or guardians.) Ninety-two percent of these were accompanied by members of their immediate family.

munications systems that permit contact with other parts of the nation, residents of Anchorage continue to believe that distance from the continental United States affects their daily lives. As a result, persons who remain in the state view their geographic isolation as the catalyst for a "forced self-reliance" in which decisions once jointly resolved become a matter of individual concern:

> There are more times here, as opposed to other places, when you have to make decisions on your own, by default. (male, 32, dentist, four years in Alaska)

> You get something in Alaska that other states don't have. You're alone up here. You have to make a go of it. (female, 37, homemaker, seventeen years in Alaska)

> A special kind of people live in Alaska. To be here you have to be special. We're all away from our families, and we have to adapt (female, 30, pharmacist, seven years in Alaska)

> It's a real challenge to raise a family in Alaska. There are no familiar ties, no relatives. It's not as easy to live here as elsewhere, and that's what makes it a challenge to be in Alaska. (male, 34, civil engineer, seven years in Alaska)

Over time, those who decide to stay in the state complain less frequently about the effects of geographic isolation, and concomitantly, their frequency of letterwriting and long-distance telephoning decreases while their number of close friends in Alaska increases.[9] This shared feeling of pride in

9. Given the number of people who mentioned isolation as a major dislike concerning life in Alaska, we obtain the following differences with respect to length of residence: less than five years, 15.8 percent; five to nine years, 22.2 percent; ten to nineteen years, 3.0 percent; twenty or more years, 11.1 percent. Also, in two different analyses of variance, frequency of contact with friends and family outside of Alaska was found to decrease with length of residence ($p < 0.05$), whereas the percentage of close friends one had living in Alaska increased with length of residence ($p < 0.001$).

a newly discovered self-reliance parallels a recognition that life in Alaska promotes a system of mutual aid in which friends come to substitute for family, a paradox similar to one noted by Boatright (1941) in his study of the nineteenth-century American frontier. "Alaska is still a place where people help each other," remarked one man who had lived in Anchorage for six years. Soon after they moved to Anchorage others realized the importance that adopting a new "family" has for newcomers:

Alaska is very much a large family. People are involved with each other. That's something I became aware of very soon after I arrived. I couldn't go back to California now and be happy. I'm 100 percent for anything up here. (female, 32, entertainer, three years in Alaska)

I've found that I've made closer friends up here than in other places we've lived. You tend to substitute them for family. (male, 24, air traffic controller, one year in Alaska)

There is a certain sense of community here. Alaska fits my philosophy of how life should be. (male, 35, computer programmer, one year in Alaska)

Given these several indications that distance from the rest of the nation influences the lives of Anchorage residents, it is reasonable to conclude that those who fail to downplay the effects of isolation or who view their isolation as the precursor to a stifling ethnocentrism rather than the source of a mandatory self-reliance are more likely to leave Alaska.[10]

10. There is no direct support for this assertion because I did not interview people who have left Alaska. I did, however, ask current residents if they knew anyone who had moved away from the state. Of those who knew someone who had moved (n=126), 25 percent thought their friends had left to be near family or friends, and another 7 percent attributed their relocation specifically to the geographic isolation of Alaska. Corroborating evidence for this statement is also found in Bardo and Bardo (1980) in their work on American migrants to Australia.

Cabin Fever: Reorientation of Time

> Winter is the watershed between people who merely live in Alaska and the real "Alaskans."
> At least that is the image that hits newcomers to Alaska. The pride of staying through the winter is so strong, recent arrivals say Alaska's veterans are "worse than Texans" about being Alaskans. (*Anchorage Times,* October 9, 1977)

These were the beginning sentences of an article on cabin fever that appeared in an Alaskan newspaper in 1977. They are not unique to 1977, for each year, as the days begin to shorten, winter becomes a newsworthy topic. What Sinclair Lewis said of the Midwest is also true of Alaska: here, winter is more an industry than a season. What appears an obsession with winter to most Outsiders is a normal topic of conversation among residents of Anchorage. Perhaps this is because there are constant reminders that winters in Alaska are different from winters in other parts of the country. At least one of the annual references to cabin fever will include a few lines of Robert Service poetry:

> This is the law of the Yukon, and ever she makes it plain:
> Send not your foolish and feeble; send me your strong and your sane—
> Strong for the red rage of battle; sane, for I harry them sore;
> Send me men girt for the combat, men who are grit to the core

If you ask Anchorage residents what they dislike most about living in Alaska, they will probably say something about their winters—not often referring to the severity of the climate, but rather to the long hours of darkness and length of the season.[11] In contrast to complaints about the

---

11. The most frequently reported dislike about living in Alaska mentioned by those interviewed (33 percent) was the length and darkness of Alaskan winters.

geographic isolation of Alaska, which decrease over time, these objections to Alaskan winters *increase* with one's length of residence, at least until one has lived in the state for over twenty years.[12] New friendships may fill the void created by relocation, but the dark winter season will not grow shorter as each year passes. Consequently, residents maintain that Outsiders don't experience the same seasonal hardships. As one local journalist commented, "People in New York don't get cabin fever, Alaskans get cabin fever. People in New York suffer from ennui."

In Service's day they called it "Arctic hysteria" or the "Aleutian stare," a raging madness prompted by long, dark days of living in a ten- by ten-foot log house. The contemporary phenomenon of cabin fever is characterized by somewhat milder symptoms: depression, lethargy, nervousness, loss of appetite, disorientation. Nevertheless, urban and rural Alaskans alike feel the pressures of everyday life intensify as the days shrink to less than six hours of sunlight and the claustrophobia associated with the isolation of Alaska becomes more pronounced. Cabin fever often begins as a vague feeling that things are "not quite right." One victim described it as "an itch you can't scratch" (Beirne, 1979). For others, cabin fever has visible manifestations:

> You can really feel "locked up" in Alaska. You have to fly out. You can't just get in your car and leave. Late in the winter I start feeling stuck. I start going crazy. (female, 36, homemaker, five years in Alaska)

> I really hate the dark of winter. It's depressing. When I wake up at 10 o'clock, it could be 10 A.M. or P.M. Because of where I work, I don't see daylight but two days a week. (female, 25, air traffic controller, six years in Alaska)

12. Complaints about the darkness and length of Alaskan winters increase with length of residence (by group) up to the point where persons have lived in Alaska for twenty years or longer: less than five years, 23.7 percent; five to nine years, 40.7 percent; ten to nineteen years, 51.5 percent; twenty years or longer, 25.0 percent.

Some groups appear to be harder hit by cabin fever than others. One therapist in Anchorage who is experienced in dealing with victims of cabin fever estimates that about two-thirds of his patients are women.[13] The homemaker who cares for small children the better part of each day often finds herself in need of a break from the monotony of housework. It becomes increasingly difficult to get out and take advantage of what little sun is available. Mothers become more protective of their children, whom they are reluctant to have stay out after dark. If the family income is low, all of these problems are compounded. Rents in Alaska are high, and those who live in trailers or small apartments find themselves particularly cramped when doors and windows must remain closed, waiting for a spring that seems forever in the distance.

In attempting to ward off the claustrophobic effects of constant hours of cold and darkness, communities in Alaska punctuate the winter with events that encourage resident participation. In February, Anchorage hosts the Fur Rendezvous, a week of dinners, dances, and sports and a chance to relive a part of the Alaskan past. In addition to providing an organized channel for resident accommodation to these seasonal variations, these events reinforce a sense of participating in a history shared exclusively by local residents. As one woman remarked, "We spend much of the winter planning for summer—kind of like a bear hibernating." Some Alaskans come out of hibernation having drunk a little more than they intended, but those who manage to "survive" really do feel a sense of achievement.[14] As these Anchorage residents put it:

13. There is some support for this statement in my survey results. Women were more likely than men to mention Alaskan winters as a major dislike concerning life in Alaska (41.7 percent compared with 30.2 percent). This difference between sexes holds when controlling for length of residence.
14. Data compiled by the Anchorage Department of Health and Environmental Protection indicate that treatment for alcohol and drug abuse is greatest during the late winter months. For quarterly statistics, see Municipality of Anchorage (1980).

I made my peace with the snow after one winter. (male, 33, architect, four years in Alaska)

I felt like an Alaskan after the first winter. If I could make it through that, I knew I could make it through another one. (male, 24, air traffic controller, one year in Alaska)

Newcomers to Anchorage, then, think of making it through a winter as another "survival test" and, like learning to cope with the physical isolation of Alaska, as a further indication of their commitment to staying in the state. Not only do these processes emphasize the uniqueness of Alaska as compared with the rest of the United States, but also they are essential in making the transition from newcomer to old-timer or, as residents might say, from Cheechako to Sourdough.

Residential Identification and Group Differentiation

Practically everyone living in Alaska today might be considered a newcomer. A transient population is nothing new to the state, and the distinction between newcomer and old-timer dates back to the gold rush days at the turn of the century. Then, as now, Cheechakos were expected to act out a particular role, to assume a certain naiveté concerning the ways of Alaska. Consider these accounts of two Cheechakos turned Sourdoughs dating from the early 1900s:

Whenever a newcomer did or said anything that outraged the Alaskan proprieties, it was excused by the half-contemptuous explanation, "Oh, he is a Cheechako and doesn't know any better." A splendid alibi and which like charity covered a multitude of sins and sheer asininity or stupidity. (Clark, 1967:249)

We were up early, and Jap and I went out to the street when we heard a shot and looked up to see a man run across the street and then drop. We hurried back and got our guns. We had 32 Stevens revolvers and put them in our pockets, and with our hands ready for action, not knowing what to expect. Soon afterwards we learned from a man that "he had it coming to him—it's a wonder he didn't get it sooner." We learned then that no matter what kind of crowd you may be in, if you keep your mouth shut and attend to your own business, you are never in danger of harm from outsiders, especially if you are Cheechakos and are broke and green as we surely showed ourselves to be. (Smith, 1967:130–131)

In earlier times Cheechakos may have been allowed a few blunders because of their unfamiliarity with Alaskan proprieties, but contemporary Sourdoughs are quite critical of new arrivals. This is largely a result of the dramatic changes in the scenery of Anchorage that occurred with the influx of population from the continental United States in recent years. Construction of the oil pipeline left visible marks on the Alaskan landscape, but it also affected those who were living in the state at the time the building began. It is not uncommon to hear these Anchorage residents bemoan the loss of simpler days.[15]

The thing I dislike most about living in Alaska is the attitude of the new people around me. Before the pipeline, I can't remember people locking their homes up. There is just not as much trust—neighborly faith—as there was before. If you used the food in someone's cabin, you replaced it the next time you were there.

15. Those who have lived in Alaska for twenty or more years are more likely to complain about the changes brought on by newcomers than are those who have lived in the state for shorter periods. Grouped according to length of residence, the percentage of people who mentioned these changes as a major dislike regarding life in Alaska were as follows: less than five years, 0.0 percent; five to nine years, 3.7 percent; ten to nineteen years, 3.0 percent; twenty or more years, 33.3 percent.

Now, everyone keeps their cabins locked. (male, 32, teacher, ten years in Alaska)

Old-time Alaskans were altogether different. They were neighborly and helped one another. People would stop to help you on the road, but that courtesy has drifted away. They won't even yield to you on the road now. It's dog eat dog, and may the best man win. (male, 74, retired, thirty years in Alaska)

It used to be that what was yours was yours. No thievery. Money would stay in your car. You never locked your cabin. You left it stocked so that others could use it. That was the "Law of the Land." Today, you don't pick up anybody who's hitchin'. We have too many "do-gooders" from the South 48, too many who are here to pick up a fast buck before leaving the country. (male, 49, maintenance foreman, twenty-six years in Alaska)

After the pipeline, we got a lot of people we couldn't assimilate. They'd pass you on the right, and drove their trucks on the tundra. They brought drugs and thievery. We were left with the feeling that we'd been robbed twice. (female, 50, homemaker, twenty-three years in Alaska)

It is doubtful whether crime or drugs or mistrust was lacking in Anchorage before the early 1970s, and it is not surprising that community members will place the blame for a great many things on strangers. Nevertheless, the many people who had recently moved to Anchorage appeared to threaten the values and beliefs that many older residents feel are the most "Alaskan" part of Alaska: an openness and friendliness with neighbors, an implicit trust of others, a respect for wilderness conditions, a commitment to stay in the state and to learn its ways. And although all of these are important, perhaps it is this last quality found lacking in newcomers that causes the most concern among contemporary Sourdoughs. Because many Cheechakos of the 1970s and 1980s are seen as unwilling to make a commitment to staying in Alaska, they are denied the "Alaskan" label and are treated more like visitors than residents.

> The boomers who came up here to make money had no intention of staying in Alaska. They had no intention of becoming Alaskans any more than a Chinaman would. (male, 56, automobile parts manager, thirteen years in Alaska)

> Newer Alaskans seem to be friendly, but they're not open. They are here for a short period of time. They know it, and we know it. (female, 36, salesperson, twenty-two years in Alaska)

> We have a lot of population turnover here, but they're not Alaskans. (male, 38, paint contractor, thirteen years in Alaska)

My survey data support these assertions to some extent in that people who had lived in Alaska for extended periods expected to stay there longer than more recent arrivals. Yet it is not clear whether these groups differed in the way they viewed the permanence of their relocation at the time they moved to Alaska.[16] Most (56 percent) of the people interviewed remembered thinking of their initial move to the state as a temporary one, with plans to stay made on a contingency basis (cf. De Amicis, 1976). Typical of this group was the comment of one newcomer who remarked, "I'll give it a couple of years and see how things work out." Anchorage landlords are well acquainted with this phenomenon, for newcomers have little trouble finding apartments that require no lease and are rented month to month.

Although long-term residents did not differ from more recent migrants in their initial plans to remain in Alaska

16. An analysis of variance involving current plans to stay in Alaska and length of residence indicated a significant difference ($p < 0.05$) among groups. A second analysis of variance involving how long respondents expected to stay at the time they moved did not result in a significant difference among groups that varied in length of residence.

temporarily, they are nevertheless reluctant to describe those around them as Alaskans. This progression toward more rigorous standards for newcomers is a response to the rapid increase in state population during the past decade. In earlier times, simply living in the state was sufficient to qualify for the status of Alaskan. But as population increased, those already living in Alaska developed other ways with which to differentiate themselves from new arrivals. Thus, standards of *place* of residence shifted to those concerning *length* of residence, and general knowledge of Alaska came to mean specific opinions regarding such things as the use of state resources. Consequently, old-timers may continue to treat others as Cheechakos, regardless of how long they have lived in Alaska.

This notion that the Alaskan label is something conferred by others is familiar to newcomers. Statements like "It looks like you've got to be here about twenty-five years before they'll let you be one" imply an understanding that designation as an Alaskan is something that must be earned.[17] Residents of the state who don't consider themselves to be Alaskans, but who wish to be thought of as such by others, feel this way because of the respect that comes with the title (cf. Strauss, 1959). One newcomer to Alaska explains:

> Old people in Alaska are respected by the young. If I had a man outside that had lived in Alaska for twenty years and I told a young man that he should talk to him, then the youngster would think that the older man had something of value to offer him. But what if I went to Chevy Chase, Maryland, and did the same thing? Do you think the youngster would have any interest in listening to the twenty-year resident of Maryland? It's just not the same. There's a certain credit given people

17. In describing the processes of mortification and transcendence, Kanter (1972) notes that communities encourage members to discard their old lives and to make attachment to the new community a central concern. Status within the group is measured by such factors as length of affiliation, with members counting their ages from the time of joining.

who have lived up here for twenty to thirty years. (male, 42, business consultant, two years in Alaska)

One need not look far to find signs of an appeal to this Alaskan image. State and local politicians rank length of residence first in their list of qualifications for office. Manufacturing and consulting firms promote their "vast experience" in dealing with Alaskan residents as a source of legitimacy. Long-term residents are entitled to a number of economic benefits, most recently higher state income tax rebates made possible by lease sales in the Beaufort Sea.[18] Length of residence in Alaska, then, has become a shorthand way of accounting for the sacrifices that accompany living in the state, such as learning to live with high prices, coping with distance from family and friends, and putting up with the long, dark winters.

Adopting the Alaskan Label

The question remains as to whether residents of Anchorage unequivocally accept the standards of those around them, for each newcomer may decide at what time and for what reasons he or she becomes an Alaskan. To some old-timers, those who were not born in Alaska or who have not spent the majority of their lives in the state will never qualify for the status of Sourdough. Despite these objections, however, few residents of Anchorage feel that they "don't have the right" to call themselves Alaskans. Almost everyone interviewed (88 percent) considered himself or herself to be an

18. Under Alaska's original "Share the Oil Wealth" program, every adult received $50 for each twelve months of residence in Alaska since statehood. Also, Alaska residents who had filed state income tax returns for at least three years did not pay taxes through 1984. In a *New York Times* article of June 15, 1980, one federal official was quoted as saying, "It seems to imply that having lived in Alaska, you have suffered." Court challenges to this original plan may call into question other state economic benefits (e.g., retirement pensions) linked to years of residence.

Alaskan, thereby discounting the possible effects of length of residence in applying this label. In fact, over two-thirds of those who thought of themselves as Alaskans began to do so within three years of moving to the state. Most residents felt that they had demonstrated their commitment to living in Alaska by that time and that one way of signifying their willingness to endure the effects of climate and isolation was to call themselves Alaskans.

Because most Anchorage residents are quick to see themselves as Alaskans, it is more instructive to inquire as to why they do so. Thus far, we have assumed that residents of Anchorage share some notion of what it means to be an Alaskan, but as Mills (1939:679) notes, it is possible for persons to "interpret the 'same' symbol differently." This qualification presents a more accurate rendering of this process as it applies to the definitions of an Alaskan employed by Anchorage residents. Their reasons for thinking of themselves as Alaskans varied, but as a group, their responses can be divided into two major categories: those common to identification with any community and those in some way peculiar to Alaska.

The first category included such things as buying a home or acquiring property in the state, establishing new friendships, voting or becoming politically active, and simply having been born in Alaska. Residents who identified as Alaskans for these kinds of reasons compose less than one-quarter (23 percent) of the people I interviewed. The remainder began to think of themselves as Alaskans for some reason unique to their experiences of living in the state: surviving a winter, going Outside and confronting others who make them realize the opportunities Alaska affords, developing an appreciation for the natural beauty of the state and participating in outdoor activities, experiencing a unique sense of community in Anchorage, and discovering that a substantial number of people display even less commitment to staying in Alaska.

I felt like an Alaskan after the first couple of years. That's when you are an Alaskan because you've lived, coped, done different things. (female, 40, homemaker, fourteen years in Alaska)

We really started to feel like Alaskans when my husband and I made a business trip Outside. They were all doing the same thing down there as when we left. We didn't want to go back to that. If you want to do something and have the guts to do it, you can do it here. (female, 40, general contractor, fourteen years in Alaska)

I felt like an Alaskan because I do so many things people who live here haven't done, like take advantage of fishing and hunting. (male, 19, military service, two years in Alaska)

I first felt like an Alaskan when the pipeline started, when the state population started to expand. I felt that way because of the others coming in. They made me feel like an Alaskan because of their newness to Alaska. (male, 35, pilot, nineteen years in Alaska)

Although they represent only a small proportion of those interviewed, some newcomers to Anchorage reported that they began to identify as Alaskans *even before* they moved to Alaska. Their remarks are revealing because they demonstrate how the expectations of migrants can shape their initial responses to Alaska as "home." The experiences of these newcomers attest to the strength that the image of Alaska as a frontier may have in initiating a "migration of selves" prior to the "migration of bodies" (cf. Maines, 1978):

I felt like an Alaskan before I crossed the Alaska border. I stopped for gas at a station about fifty or sixty miles from Haines [Alaska]. The man there took one look at my Michigan plates and said, "Son, it looks like you're a long way from home." I answered, "No, sir. I'm home now." (male, 38, municipal tax assessor, nine years in Alaska)

[I first felt like an Alaskan] ten minutes after I stepped off of the plane. No, even before that, when I was flying into Anchorage. I knew I was going to love it here even before I got here. I was struck by the natural beauty of Alaska. (male, 36, military service, three years in Alaska)

Interestingly, there are no significant differences with respect to several group characteristics—sex, education, occupation, length of residence—between those who see themselves as Alaskan for some reason unique to the state and those who do not, nor is there variation between the two groups as to the length of time which passes before they begin to think of themselves as Alaskans.[19] It seems reasonable to conclude, then, that "becoming an Alaskan" is a process familiar to most of those who stay in Alaska for even a short period of time and that the final step in this process involved having "earned" the right to think of oneself as an Alaskan.

Thus, as residents of Anchorage distinguish between themselves and Outsiders (the topic of Chapter 3), they also have ways of distinguishing themselves from other community members. In the former instance, Outsiders are different from state residents because they haven't lived in Alaska. In the latter, some residents are not "real" Alaskans because they haven't lived in the state long enough. But how long is "long enough"?

The analysis in this chapter supports the general proposition that high rates of community in- and out-migration promote residential identification. As illustrated in the case of newcomers to Anchorage, rapid population turnover results in a relatively low average length of residence, along with a small number of non-Native adults who were born in Alaska. Regardless of how long they have lived in the state, almost all residents will find several who have arrived even

19. The only exception is age. Residents between thirty and thirty-nine years old were more likely to feel like Alaskans for reasons peculiar to the state than were those either younger or older. (This relationship persists when controlling for length of residence.)

more recently, as well as many who, having spent only a few years in Alaska, have already returned to the continental United States. This population turnover allows newcomers to Anchorage to discount the protests of older residents who might challenge their claims to community membership. In viewing more recent arrivals as their group of reference, Anchorage residents begin to think of themselves as Alaskans long before they have spent twenty years in the state. And as long as this pattern of migration persists, we can expect Anchorage residents to achieve a sense of place by making comparisons among themselves.

CHAPTER 5

The Marketing of Alaska

I want Alaska to be a dream come true, like the feeling you get after watching a *National Geographic* special, or anything that touches your heart. Things like this happen seldom; they should happen every day. The search for individualism and independence has got to be a constant thing, a *marketed* thing. Never let up on it. A snowballing thing that we can't help but talk about. (statement made by Bob Uchitel during a planning session for "Alaska '84")

Despite the ease with which great distances are bridged today, the remoteness of Alaska continues to place the state beyond the reach of most Americans. Few residents of the continental United States will ever visit Alaska; fewer still will ever live there. But visitors and migrants to Alaska, along with a much larger group of Americans, possess some image of Alaska linking it to its frontier heritage. How they acquire this image is largely a matter of the structure of information flows, and the content of the frontier image is itself subject to strategies of information management. Because both the acquisition and content of Alaska's frontier image are open to manipulation, those interested in marketing Alaska to outsiders have been able to profit from the instrumental production of a frontier ideology apart from verifiable experience.

This suggests that the frontier image of Alaska has been "commodified," to borrow the term used by others to describe the transformation of an image into products of exchange. Goldman and Dickens (1983:585) define the "*com-*

modification of the rural myth" as the "packaging of the images and value system of rural life as if they are contained in the commodity with which they are being associated." An analogous commodification of the *frontier* myth is clearly recognizable in the advertising campaigns of the Alaska tourist industry. Visitors to Alaska are promised a once-in-a-lifetime pioneering experience that will follow them the rest of their lives. As a recent travel poster asserted, "Once you've gone to Alaska, you never come all the way back." The temporary nature of tourism makes it particularly well suited to techniques of information control.

In a similar way, those who will never venture north are encouraged to participate in the renewal of spirit that forms a part of the frontier myth. Travel magazines depicting the wilder side of Alaskan life reinforce the image of the forty-ninth state as the last American frontier. And a recent (yet failed) attempt to take the spirit of Alaska on the road in the form of a Broadway musical was but another step toward offering the independent qualities of the frontier myth as a solution to regaining individual autonomy.

Although it does not imply the same measure of overt information control, migration to Alaska is also shaped by the frontier imagery surrounding the state. Few newcomers bring with them a realistic sense of daily life in Anchorage, which is not surprising given the limited contact most migrants have with Alaska. But at the same time that new-found realities may not measure up to expectations, the exotic imagery associated with Alaska plays a large role in attracting migrants. Without it, one might expect Alaska to be passed over as a potential migration destination. In choosing Alaska, migrants are often responding to the "call of the wild."

This chapter takes a closer look at each of these groups—migrants, visitors, and avid fans—as targets of or responses to the commodification of the frontier myth. In doing so, it becomes clear that its frontier image remains one of Alaska's most valuable resources.

The Call of the Wild:
Migration to Alaska

It is perhaps too easy to dismiss the frontier images surrounding Alaska as ephemeral qualities that exist only as
the fantasies of would-be pioneers. Yet it is impossible to
understand migration to Alaska without according these
images a prominent place in that discussion. Along with their
luggage, newcomers to Anchorage bring with them expectations of a more exotic life, a fact closely tied to the sources
of information available to potential migrants. Unlike others
who move within the continental United States, few migrants
to Alaska have kinship and friendship networks that provide
them with information and assistance in moving. In the
absence of these networks, they rely on secondary channels,
which portray Alaska as the last American frontier. As a
result, newcomers to Anchorage come to describe their
relocation in the imagery of pioneering self-reliance.

More important, the viability of Alaska as a migration
destination is sustained by its wilderness image. Although
frontiers have long been associated with economic gain in
this country, the considerable expense required to move to
Alaska means that migration to the state is seldom, if ever,
justified in monetary terms alone. Without its appeal as one
of the few remaining places where wilderness areas are
readily accessible, Alaska would most likely be passed over
by those who are considering relocating.

In short, migration to Alaska is deeply interwoven with
the symbolism surrounding the American frontier. Among
the tangible results of this apparently intangible image is the
role it plays in attracting newcomers to Anchorage.

Sources of Information and Assistance

Family and friendship networks have been the focus of many
demographic studies, not only because they have been shown
to influence decisions to move, but also because they affect

post-migration adjustment (Ritchey, 1976). Friends and family members may encourage migration by providing information about economic opportunities or social conditions elsewhere (Bieder, 1973; Brown, Schwarzweller, and Mangalam, 1963; Choldin, 1973; Litwak, 1960), or they may direct migration by providing aid or assistance at the new place of residence (Bogue, 1977; Brown, Schwarzweller, and Mangalam, 1963; Choldin, 1973; Litwak, 1960).

Because few newcomers have family or friends living in Alaska when they move, social ties play an insignificant role in the process of migration to Anchorage. Almost half (47 percent) reported that they did not know anyone residing in Alaska at the time they moved. Of the 53 percent who reported having ties to the state, about 25 percent had family members currently living in Anchorage, 19 percent had friends living there, and the remaining 9 percent had relatives or friends living elsewhere in the state when they moved.[1]

These results run counter to previous findings linking social ties to patterns of migration. Lansing and Mueller (1967) report that approximately half of all moves are to areas where migrants have family and that over two-thirds are to places where migrants have friends. Choldin (1973) notes that 68 percent of migrants to Chicago are met by someone (usually relatives) when they arrive. Similar results are found in Price's (1971) study of urban migration and Tilly and Brown's (1968) work on migration to Wilmington, Delaware.[2]

In the absence of friends or family at their destination, migrants to Anchorage appear to receive assistance only from those travelling with them. Two-thirds of the sample moved to Alaska with at least one other person, and ninety-

1. Only two respondents reported that they had both family and friends living in Alaska at the time they migrated. Because of this small number, they are included with the percentage reporting family members living in Alaska at the time of move.

2. These comparisons are even more striking considering respondents in the Anchorage sample were reporting friends or family members living *anywhere* in Alaska.

two percent of these were accompanied by members of their immediate families, usually their spouses and children. Because most new arrivals find that the only people they know are those who come with them, they typically view migration to Alaska as the catalyst for an imposed self-reliance. As noted in Chapter 4, this serves as an important anchor for self and community identity among new arrivals to Anchorage.

Just as migrants to Anchorage find alternative sources of assistance in the absence of ties to current residents, they receive information about Alaska through various secondary networks. When asked to recall the sources of information about Alaska they received prior to moving to Anchorage, 42 percent of the respondents reported that their expectations about life in Anchorage were shaped by the media: magazine articles or books they had read or movies they had seen. Only 25 percent had obtained information about Alaska through visiting the state prior to moving, and fewer still (22 percent) had talked to someone who had visited Alaska. As expected, only a small number (9 percent) had received information from current state residents. Another 10 percent cited either school instruction or the mere knowledge of Alaska's geographic location as their source of information.[3]

The source of information on which Alaskan migrants draw appears to influence the expectations they harbor prior to moving, as well as the extent to which these expectations are met once they arrive. The assumption that one's life will, in some ways, change as a result of relocating is implied in the general "pull" model of migration. Not surprisingly, then, almost everyone interviewed (92 percent) reported that he or she thought life in Anchorage would differ from that of his or her previous residence. The content of these expectations is presented in Table 5.1.

3. Percentages will not sum up to 100 percent because respondents could cite more than one source of information about Alaska. These percentages are based on a sample size of ninety-seven.

Table 5.1. Migrant Expectations Concerning Life in Alaska*

Type of Expectation	Percent
Wilderness-related	**80**
Primitive/isolated	53
Harsh climate	33
Access to wilderness	17
Exciting, adventure	5
Lifestyle-related	**29**
Rural atmosphere	13
Relaxed lifestyle	10
Greater personal freedom	8
Friendly people	6
Economic-related	**20**
Greater economic opportunity	10
Higher cost of living	6
Urban factors resulting from large population	5

*Percentages will not sum to 100 percent because of multiple response; n = 97.

The most frequently mentioned preconceptions of migrants to Anchorage were descriptive of wilderness aspects of the state. Eighty percent mentioned factors pertaining to expected differences in climate or terrain, with most expecting Anchorage to be an isolated frontier outpost lacking many of the modern conveniences found in other urban areas of the United States.[4] Substantially fewer (29 percent) expected a change in lifestyle, a return to a slower-paced environment

4. To see if this emphasis on wilderness qualities has changed over time, length of residence was introduced as a control variable. The results suggest that wilderness expectations far outweigh those relating to lifestyle or economics, regardless of when the respondent moved to Alaska.

where people are friendlier and personal independence is high. An even smaller number (20 percent) anticipated economic changes involving greater financial opportunity and a higher cost of living.[5]

Comparing the content of migrant expectations with their source demonstrates that what newcomers know about Alaska is closely linked to where they obtained their information. Table 5.2 shows that expectations concerning wilderness and lifestyle aspects of the state were carried primarily through the media, whereas expectations regarding economic differences were largely a result of personal networks. These findings suggest a continuing tradition of journalistic preoccupation with the rougher and larger-than-life aspects of American frontiers. By contrast, only some measure of personal contact appeared to broaden the expectations of Anchorage migrants to include a more varied (and, in some cases, a more realistic) perspective on contemporary Alaskan life.

As respondents were currently living in Alaska, they were asked to compare their previous expectations about the state with their subsequent experiences. In retrospect, how accurate were the opinions of Anchorage residents before they moved? Although over half (55 percent) thought that their preconceptions were either extremely or somewhat accurate, the reported accuracy of their expectations varied with respect to the type of change they anticipated. As shown in Table 5.3, those who anticipated either lifestyle or economic changes were considerably less surprised by what they found in Alaska than were those who expected changes involving wilderness qualities. The most widely publicized facets of

5. Because respondents were allowed to mention more than one expected difference, the types of expectations were crosstabulated with each other to determine if the distributions of the three variables were significantly different. The results indicate that those who expected wilderness conditions were not likely to mention economic or lifestyle conditions, whereas it was likely that those mentioning lifestyle changes would also mention economic changes.

Table 5.2. Type of Expectation by Source of Information About Alaska*

Type of Expectation	Media (books, movies, etc.) (Percent)	Personal Visit (Percent)	Visitors (Percent)	Current Residents (Percent)	Geographic Location (Percent)	School Instruction (Percent)
Wilderness-related	50.0	19.2	20.5	5.1	6.4	5.1
Lifestyle-related	38.5	26.9	26.9	15.4	3.8	0.0
Economic-related	21.1	42.1	26.3	26.3	5.3	0.0

*Percentages will not sum to 100 percent because of multiple response; n = 97.

Table 5.3. Mean Values for Accuracy of Expectations Judged by Migrants to Anchorage

Type of Expectation	Mean* (n)
Lifestyle-related	3.8 (27)
Economic-related	3.5 (19)
Wilderness-related	2.8 (78)

*Means are given from a five-point Likert scale response (extremely accurate to not at all accurate) to the following question: "Thinking back on it now, do you think that the ideas you had about Alaska before you came were accurate?" A higher mean value indicates that the respondent felt that his or her expectations were more, rather than less, accurate once he or she arrived.

Alaskan life—and those most frequently expected by new-comers—were thought to be incongruous with the realities of everyday life in Anchorage. Two migrants to Anchorage expressed this irony clearly:

I thought Alaska would be the "last frontier," the last place where people haven't been established for hundreds of years. It's what the Old West must have been like in the 1880s, a place where everyone came from someplace else. After I came to Alaska, I found this to be true. But the frontier with its wide open spaces was not so wide open. There's a lot of land here, but it's difficult to get anywhere. (male, 36, petroleum engineer, three years in Alaska)

I didn't dream that it would be like it was when we came to Alaska. I thought we'd be living on a private lake, secluded. We never found that here. I suppose those were pretty fanciful ideas. (male, 48, manager, eleven years in Alaska)

An interesting corollary to these findings involves whether migrants to Anchorage knew a visitor to or a resident of the state when they moved. Having talked to a visitor prior to moving to Anchorage had little effect on the accuracy of migrant expectations. By contrast, contact with a resident prior to moving was a significant factor in bringing expectations into line with the realities of life in Anchorage.[6] This suggests that the small amount of time visitors spend in the state is not sufficient to assess the practical realities of living in Anchorage. Tourism, in general, provides an incomplete rendering of the countless everyday events that are the stuff of community life. As one student of the subject notes:

> The tourist sees the country he visits too much in terms of its superficially picturesque, the predictably "exotic" or "typical" aspects and experiences of local life but highly selectively and episodically. The shorter he stays the worse the distortion. (Lengyel, 1975)

Adding to this the efforts of the tourist industry to capitalize on the state's wilderness image (a topic to be addressed shortly), it is not surprising that current residents of Alaska provide more valid information to migrants than do visitors.

Reasons for Moving

Just as the wilderness imagery associated with Alaska plays a significant role in shaping the expectations of Anchorage migrants, it also contributes to their decisions to relocate. Respondents to the Anchorage survey were asked to rate a number of reasons for coming to Alaska, from extremely to not at all important using Likert-type scale items. (See Table 5.4). As a group, they valued Alaska most highly as a place characterized by personal independence and opportunity. This was followed in importance by employment-related factors, the desire to be close to a wilderness environment,

---

6. These conclusions are based on two difference of means tests: for knowing visitors: $t = 0.55$, $df = 95$, n.s.; for knowing residents: $t = 2.72$, $df = 95$, $p < .01$.

Table 5.4. Mean Values for Responses to Reasons for Moving to Alaska

Reason*	Mean
A chance to be independent, to start something new	3.51
A challenge, an exciting job	3.16
To be close to a wilderness environment	3.07
Curiosity about Alaska	2.96
Long-term economic opportunity	2.69
To get away from urban problems	2.65
Immediate income gains	2.57
To live a pioneer's life, to be self-reliant	2.02
To be with family and/or friends	1.79
To go to school, be in the military	1.71

*Reasons for moving to Alaska are listed in decreasing order of importance. A higher mean score indicates a more important reason for moving to Alaska.

and simple curiosity about Alaska. Other factors figured less prominently into migration decisions.

In Table 5.4 the eight most important reasons for moving to Alaska can be meaningfully divided into two groups: economic and non-economic.[7] Economic reasons include "a

7. This particular grouping, as well as the decision to analyze only eight of the ten reasons for moving to Alaska, was based on a factor analysis of all ten reasons for moving to Alaska. In this factor analysis, the first eight reasons were distributed by substantial loadings between two factors. Highly loaded variables on the first factor included "a chance to be independent, start something new" (0.568), "a challenge, an exciting job" (0.683), "long-term economic opportunity" (0.631), and "immediate income gains" (0.692). Collectively, these four reasons represent an emphasis on economic con-

chance to be independent, to start something new," "a challenge, an exciting job," "long-term economic opportunity," and "immediate income gains." The non-economic reasons include "to be close to a wilderness environment," "curiosity about Alaska," "to get away from urban problems," and "to live a pioneer's life, to be self-reliant." As the previous discussion would lead one to expect, these non-economic reasons for moving are in some way related to the frontier imagery associated with Alaska. The desire to be near family and friends, a major non-economic reason for moving documented elsewhere (Long and Hansen, 1979; Berardo, 1967), is rated ninth out of the ten factors shown here, with a corresponding group mean of 1.79. Where non-economic factors are concerned, Alaska appeals to many newcomers through its wilderness qualities, an attraction undocumented in migration studies conducted elsewhere in the United States.

Anchorage migrants sometimes viewed these two kinds of reasons for moving to Alaska as complementary factors. One man in his thirties who had lived in Alaska three years described the state as "the best of both worlds. It allows us the opportunity to be outdoors, while at the same time the economic opportunities here are great."

For others, however, one set of factors, either economic or wilderness related, was more influential in attracting them to Alaska. I pursued this distinction between economic and

siderations in deciding to move to Alaska. As "a chance to be independent, to start something new" loaded onto the same factor as other economic variables, this reason for moving can be interpreted as "a chance to be *financially* independent, to start a new *job or business.*"

The remaining four non-economic reasons for moving loaded onto a second factor: "to be close to a wilderness environment" (0.794), "curiosity about Alaska" (0.363), "to get away from urban problems" (0.516), and "to live a pioneer's life, to be self-reliant" (0.480). Because the last two reasons for moving ("nearness to family and friends," "to go to school or be in the military") did not produce substantial loadings on any factor, they were omitted from the analysis.

non-economic reasons for moving to Alaska by searching for factors that might explain a migrant's preference for one set of reasons over another. This was accomplished by constructing two additive indices—one measuring the extent to which a respondent moved for economic reasons and one measuring the extent to which the move was based on non-economic, wilderness-related factors—which were then employed as dependent variables in two regression equations. (See Table 5.5.) Three sets of factors thought to

Table 5.5. Determinants of Preference for Economic- and Wilderness-Related Reasons for Moving

Variable	Economic Reasons Index b (Standard Error)	β	Wilderness Reasons Index b (Standard Error)	β
Age at time of move	.002 (.011)	.016	−.010 (.010)	−.097
Sex (1 = male)	.276 (.190)	.144	.234 (.170)	.131
Education	.075† (.034)	.229	.018 (.031)	.060
Decision to move*	.106 (.062)	.167	.211‡ (.056)	.356
Knew visitor? (1 = yes)	.024 (.182)	.013	.070 (.163)	.043
Knew resident? (1 = yes)	.277 (.182)	.151	.054 (.163)	−.031
Length of residence	−.009 (.012)	−.085	−.026† (.010)	−.253
Constant	−.122		.522	
R²	.160†		.219§	

*Question addresses the extent to which a respondent felt that the decision to move was a matter of personal choice, rather than a result of circumstances beyond one's control. A high score on this variable indicates a large measure of personal choice.
†p<0.05, two-tailed test.
‡p<0.001, two-tailed test.
§p<0.01.

influence a migrant's emphasis on one type of reason versus the other were used as explanatory variables in this analysis: group traits that are regularly employed as migration differentials (sex, education, and age at time of move);[8] a measure of a migrant's commitment to the move (i.e., the degree of personal responsibility taken in making the decision to move); and two measures of previous contact with the state (whether the migrant knew a resident or visitor of Alaska prior to moving). Length of residence was also introduced as an additional control in both regressions.

Considering the first group of migrant characteristics, age has little effect on the degree of importance accorded economic or wilderness reasons for moving to Alaska. Although the difference in effect is slight and non-significant, the direction of effect differs in the equations. Age varies inversely with a stress on wilderness reasons for moving, a possible indication of a greater attention to Alaska's frontier qualities among younger migrants.

When sex is employed as an independent variable, men score higher on both indices than do women. Regardless of what reasons for moving are chosen, women tend to offer more moderate responses than men. Education shows a similar direct association with both indices; however, it exerts a significant independent effect only in the economic equation. In fact, education accounts for the largest proportion of variation explained by a single variable in this equation (4.8 percent). Thus, economic benefits often associated with employment opportunities in Alaska appear to be of greater concern to those better educated.

The fourth independent variable in Table 5.5 addresses the migrant's commitment to the move. Those who viewed their move to Alaska as more a matter of personal choice may be thought of as more committed to migrating in the sense that

8. Because the sample is almost exclusively white (95 percent), race is not used as an explanatory variable in this analysis. Also, introducing occupational status into these equations did not contribute to the proportion of variation explained in either index. It is therefore excluded from the presentation of results.

their psychic investment in moving is greater than those who moved in response to other circumstances. Defined in these terms, greater commitment is positively associated with an emphasis on both economic and wilderness-related reasons for moving, although these associations are not of equal significance or magnitude. This variable exerts a significant independent effect in the equation specifying wilderness factors and accounts for the largest relative contribution of any variable in this equation.[9] Any conclusion based on this comparison is at best speculative, but it perhaps suggests that migration for non-economic reasons may be associated with a greater psychic investment than that prompted by economic concerns.

Although contact with a visitor fails to describe a significant effect in either equation, knowing a resident exerts a substantial, though non-significant, positive effect on moving for economic reasons. This finding corresponds to the previous analysis of migrant expectations: contact with a resident of Alaska serves as a major source of expectations that are economic in content. As such, these results support the information hypothesis (Ritchey, 1976), which suggests that established residents provide knowledge of economic opportunities to migrants. Such ties, however, have a minimal, negative impact on reasons for moving that emphasize the wilderness aspects of Alaska. Contact with a resident prior to moving decreases the extent to which a migrant stresses these non-economic factors in making the decision to move.

Finally, length of residence shows a significant inverse association with the wilderness index, while its effect in the economic equation is minimal. This may indicate that economic considerations have always been a focal concern of those moving to Alaska; American frontiers have long been cloaked in the imagery of economic opportunity and

9. The proportion of variation explained by the commitment variable in the wilderness equation is 0.122 compared with 0.043 in the economic index equation.

progress. The desire to move to Alaska for wilderness-related reasons, however, may be of more recent origin. In the face of increasing urbanization in other parts of the United States, migrants may view Alaska as one of the few remaining places where an alternative lifestyle is possible. Although the choice of Anchorage as a destination may reflect a specific concern with Alaska's wilderness image, these data direct attention to the general question regarding the variant forms that non-economic factors may assume in directing patterns of migration. If persons are considering other destinations within the United States when they move to Alaska, it is likely that Anchorage will represent the destination farthest from the migrant's point of origin, regardless of where that might be. Consequently, it is reasonable to assume that factors other than a new job or a higher salary will figure prominently into decisions to move to Alaska. For migrants to Anchorage, these may well be associated with a promise of adventure and excitement interwoven in the cultural symbolism of the "last American frontier." One woman who had recently moved to Alaska to accept a position in an Anchorage law firm addressed this issue directly:

> Why do people come to frontiers? Why would anyone want to be an attorney in Anchorage? I'm trying to find something unique about Alaska for *me*. If there's not anything here, I'd be a fool to stay. I can have material things—and more of them—anywhere. So, I'm looking for the wild, the exotic, the adventurous. (female, 26, attorney, six months in Alaska)

Thus, just as a set of frontier symbols fosters a sense of place among Anchorage residents (as described in Chapter 4), they also act to draw migrants to Alaska. In a similar way, other American cities, such as San Francisco, New Orleans, Houston, or Boston, may attract migrants because of their association with a set of unique cultural images (cf. Strauss, 1976). Further research that explores this question would not only assist in refining our understanding of the complexities involved in the decision to migrate, but would also add to our knowledge concerning the role of secondary channels in providing information to migrants. For these reasons, I will return to issues regarding the symbolic role of place in the next chapter.

The Call of the Semi-Wild:
Tourism in Alaska

By definition, touristic experiences are moments generated out of context. This does not mean that they are in any sense artificial, but it does mean that travel is a commodity that can be readily manipulated. Owing to its temporary nature, tourism necessarily provides a superficial view of new surroundings. A number of students of tourism have forcefully argued that visitors expect little more than this, and given the intrusion that such activities impose on "natives," it is unrealistic to expect them to offer anything more.

In a manner analogous to that of migrants to Anchorage, the considerable distance of Alaska from the continental United States does much to shape the content of the frontier image presented to potential visitors. The relatively non-competitive position of Alaska in the tourism market is a result of the expense required to reach the state, as well as the costs associated with visiting once there. Just as it holds forth the promise of exotic opportunities to potential migrants, Alaska—or more accurately, those seeking to promote tourism in Alaska—must offer something special to prospective visitors. What they purport to offer tourists is a once-in-a-lifetime frontier experience.

Obviously, such information management strategies are not unique to Alaska; tourism is rooted in the search for experiences that transcend the everyday. Its appeal rests both on the familiarity of the routine and on the attractiveness of other worlds. In a comparison of the two, tourism embodies the quest for the exotic and celebrates the virtues of discovery and adventure. Some have even likened the touristic journey to a "sacred" experience in Durkheimian terms, as it is associated with several values embraced by Western culture. As one student of tourism remarked:

> For Westerners who value individualism, self-reliance, and the work ethic, tourism is the *best* kind of life for it is sacred in the sense of being exciting, renewing and inherently self-fulfilling. . . . The rewards of modern tourism are phrased in terms of values we now hold up for worship: mental and physical health, social status, and diverse, exotic experiences. (Graburn, 1977:23–24)

Although Americans respond to the lure of any number of far-away places each year, Alaska is distinguished from other tourist destinations in that the qualities of individualism and self-reliance that are associated with tourism are also embodied in the myth of the American frontier. It is the "pioneering spirit" of travellers to which the Alaska tourist agent appeals, thereby depicting the journey to a frontier as the *ultimate* touristic experience.

The claim to Alaska's uniqueness as a vacation destination rests in its portrayal as a combination of many exotic places and, therefore, as a land of great contrast. This comparison is phrased primarily in terms descriptive of the geographic diversity of the state. Thus, for example, one Alaska travel brochure declared:

> Experienced travelers say that Alaska is like no other place on earth! It's a spectacular blending of the dazzling peaks of the Himalayas, the tranquil fjords of Norway, the mammoth glaciers of Antarctica, the pristine farmlands of New Zealand, the untrammeled wildlife refuges of Africa, and the frontier towns of Australia's outback.

Here, Alaska is described as a five-continent tour rolled into one seven-day vacation. This variation of climate and terrain forms the core of appeals to prospective tourists, but Alaskan tourism has also been marketed in other ways. Along with "environmental tourism," Smith (1977:2–3) identifies four other forms of tourism, each of which is incorporated in some way into outside appeals to potential visitors.

Ethnic tourism involves marketing the exotic qualities of indigenous populations. Activities of this type range from visits to remote Native villages to shopping for primitive artifacts near more populous areas of Alaska. The value of ethnic touristic experiences increases with the distance from major population centers like Anchorage; for that reason, they are often the most expensive form of tourism. *Cultural tourism,* which is closely aligned with ethnic tourism, consists of packaging a unique or perhaps vanishing lifestyle. In Alaska, this consists of numerous performances reminiscent of the rustic days of the Alaskan gold rush. *Historical tourism* involves a search for the glories of the past. Activities focus on an era now past, such as the days of the Russian colonization of Alaska and the early settlement of the state's principal cities. Lastly, *recreational tourism* includes activities that are directed toward participating in the local environment. In Alaska, this means that the glaciers, mountains, and streams are meant for hiking, backpacking, and fishing as well as for sightseeing.

These multiple images of Alaska form the basis of appeals to tourists. The diversity of touristic experiences is clearly emphasized in this single paragraph excerpted from a guidebook advertising cruises to Alaska:

We have found that visitors come to Alaska primarily to experience its fantastic scenic beauty, particularly that of the mountains, glaciers, and waterways [environmental]. In addition, many visitors wish to experience Alaska's unique history [historical] and diversity of cultures [ethnic, cultural]. Some visitors just want to draw a breath of its crisp, fragrant air or savor fresh king salmon barbecued over an open alderwood fire. Other visitors want to participate in activities in Alaska's rugged, pristine nature, whether from a sight-seeing plane or eyeball-to-eyeball with icebergs in a whitewater river raft [recreational].

No matter what the preference, such advertisements suggest that Alaska offers something to everyone and that Alaska may be just as exciting from a distance as it is up close. Like the Anchorage resident who described his Alaska experience as "pseudo-pioneering," the visitor to Alaska is offered a comfortable, relaxing, safe wilderness experience. One travel agency put the matter simply when it suggested, "Getting away from it all doesn't mean doing without."[10]

It comes as no surprise to find that Anchorage is the center for tourism in Alaska. Given the economic primacy of the state's largest city discussed in Chapter 2, one would hardly expect the tourist industry to be immune to the magnetic attraction Anchorage imposes on other Alaskan enterprises. But although economic centrality is certainly a part of the explanation, it is in no way a complete one. Rather, the concentration of goods and services in Anchorage has provided the foundation necessary to make tourism in Alaska "big business." The variety of urban amenities available to visitors makes Anchorage a viable target for mass tourism, and its proximity to wilderness recreational activities ensures a safe measure of the frontier experience. This "best of both worlds" imagery informs the local tourist publications: "Anchorage: All of Alaska is right in the neighborhood."

One of the most vivid illustrations mixing the savage with the urbane appeared in a 1980 issue of *Vogue* magazine. In an eight-page color advertisement for "Alaska! America's greatest travel adventure and the prophetic new vacation," attractive men and women—none of whom look older than

10. The theme of the ease with which travel may be accomplished is recurrent in the literature on tourism. Boorstin's (1961) polemic provides a representative example.

forty—are captured in provocative poses: a woman scrutinizing a possible purchase at an Anchorage art gallery; a couple dressed in trench coats standing atop a segment of the pipeline; a bikini-clad woman eyeing her mountain-climber friend as they frolic on a glacier. The visual images are surpassed only by the accompanying narrative.

The image of Alaska has changed. Who would have thought we would be gallery-hopping in Anchorage? Here are the images . . . some of the infinite images . . . of Alaska. A window to the ancient wisdom of the Eskimo. An abstract of the midnight sun. And ourselves. Who would have thought we'd be sporting a tan we caught skiing on a glacier? Glaciers, yes and hot springs. Bawdy bars, yes and museums. Wilderness, yes and sophistication. Alaska is our discovery, the most exciting set of extremes in the '80s. Being here, we are in the State of the next decade.

The Pipeline. Feel the energy. The light of cities. The power for factories. The roar of jets and the rush of traffic. It all begins here. The silver snake twists its way through canyons, over mountains, under rivers, past solitary bears and herds of caribou to the North Slope. And Black Gold, superheated, comes surging back over 800 miles of frozen tundra. Next time you flick out your nightlight, think of this.

Challenge met. Summit conquered. We're here, half-naked on an ice-field and loving it. It's called Ruth Glacier (lovely name for an icedream). What we thought was cold is bracing. What we thought was high is exalting. Behind us looms 20,320 feet of Mount McKinley, the literal pinnacle of the United States. Gooseflesh? Only from excitement.

But does this recasting of the frontier image of Alaska represent anything more than blatant exploitation of the pioneer nostalgia associated with the state? If pioneering requires a strong measure of adventure, self-reliance, and courage, can the "Anchorage experience" in any way approximate the frontier ideal? The answers to these questions are found in the processes of comparison that I have claimed are essential to understanding the meaning of the frontier in contemporary America. Alaska need not be a land of outhouses and log cabins in order to attract tourists longing for a taste of the primitive. It is sufficient that it provide some measure of *relative* wildness compared with other areas of the country.

Phrased in this manner, tourism in Alaska is yet another variation on the theme of how urbanization creates, in effect, an appreciation of the non-urban. Such an interpretation is not unique to frontiers but is consistent with a central irony that permeates the history of travel. When Alaska was a good deal "rougher," no one was interested in touring it. In fact, analysts concerned with fostering tourism assumed that the primitive accommodations available to visitors were the primary reason so few people travelled to Alaska.[11] Much of their concern was tied to the considerable expense required to visit Alaska. This single factor has done more to shape the composition of the visitor population than any other. Today, visitors to Alaska continue to be wealthier, older, better educated, and more likely to work in white-collar occupations than other travellers in the United States. (See Table 5.6.) Thus, just as migrants to the state represent a peculiar subset of American movers, so visitors to Alaska are drawn from a narrow segment of American travellers. But unlike newcomers to the state, visitors lay no claim to being Alaskans, and, as a result, receive a warm welcome from many state residents.

Tourists are also a welcome sight because they represent continued economic viability in Alaska. Because Alaska is known for its inability to support stable industry and because tourism is a major business in the state, many Alaskans would like to see the number of visitors increase.

11. The great number of travelogues published near the middle of this century devoted to dispelling such "myths" attests to this fact.

Table 5.6. Selected Characteristics of Travellers, Alaska and the United States

Characteristic	Alaska* (Percent)	United States† (Percent)
Sex:		
Male	67	49
Female	33	51
Age:		
18–34	33	42
35–54	45	35
55 and over	22	23
Education:		
Less than high school	5	17
High school	21	40
Some college or more	74	43
Income:		
$15,000 or less	9	40
$15,000–$24,999	13	34
$25,000 or more	78	26
Occupation:		
White collar	67	46
Blue collar	8	35
Other	25	19

*Source: Anchorage Convention and Visitors Bureau, *1982 Anchorage Visitors Survey*, Anchorage, AK., March, 1983.
†Source: Ziff-Davis Publishing Company, *Travel Market Yearbook*, Cherry Hill, NJ.: 1980.

According to a visitor's survey conducted from October, 1982, to September, 1983, approximately 650,000 non-resident visitors came to Alaska spending about $1 billion on their trips, resulting in nearly 9,000 direct visitor-related jobs (Alaska Department of Labor, 1984).

Part of the plan to broaden the spectrum of tourists to Alaska involves directly manipulating the image of Alaska as a frontier. A recent step in that direction came from an Anchorage resident who had visions of hosting the 1984 World's Fair in the state—"Alaska '84." His efforts, and the discussions surrounding this attempt, are instructive because they clearly illustrate the "commodification of the frontier myth" (cf. Goldman and Dickens, 1983) in the marketing of Alaskan tourism.

Bob Uchitel and Alaska '84

Bob Uchitel is an Alaskan success story. As a boy, he worked in his father's El Morocco Restaurant in New York, and before moving to Alaska when he was twenty-five, he worked as many other things: a dishwasher, a tour guide at Yellowstone National Park, a wildlife photographer for a television program, a heavy equipment operator, a shopping center manager. When I met him in 1979, Uchitel was still pursuing a number of interests. He was chairman of the board of Visions, a cable television network; president of Multi-Visions, the cable franchise serving Anchorage; and owner of the Uchitel Company, a heavy equipment construction firm, to mention only the larger of his professional affiliations. Alaska '84 was but another venture for this Anchorage entrepreneur who had successfully turned his stay in Alaska into an economic bonanza.[12]

Bob Uchitel's Alaska '84 had several ambitious goals, among them to "show the unique qualities of Alaska to others," "promote individualism in 'Orwell's year,'" and "export the Alaska lifestyle." He believes that Alaska is like no other place, and that if you can get people to visit the state, they will take a little of the frontier back with them:

There is a tremendous amount of potential in all of us, and Alaska seems to pull out a certain sameness in each

12. This discussion of Bob Uchitel and Alaska '84 draws on a variety of sources: attendance at public planning meetings for the fair, conversations with Uchitel and other Alaska '84 board members, and numerous articles from the *Anchorage Daily News.*

of us. Even if people don't make Alaska their home—even if they just come for a short period of time—by the time they leave they have been molded by the Alaskan spirit. Everyone is affected by it, even if they hate it when they're here.

To Uchitel, Alaska '84 would be a chance for Alaskans to "show off their superiority, to show that they are livers of life." "We think that if there's one place in the world that stands for the opposite of Orwell's Big Brother, it's Alaska," he boasts. "The individual is king in Alaska." Because he asserts that there is a bit of "Alaska" in everyone, Uchitel is optimistic about the problems that plague the country today. In fact, he claims that the solutions to many of our problems may be found in looking "north to the future."

A lot of Outsiders who visit the state see Alaska in terms of "If I was only twenty years younger." By and large, the grass is greener here. But too often we don't have the guts to make it happen ourselves. Yet we can make it a reality. Not so in California. If myth can come to equal reality, the other people will learn by our example. "If they can do it in Alaska, why can't we do it in Ohio, Paris, etc.?" We are in a position to change the world, to show others a better way. We are representatives of how the world should be.

In April, 1980, Alaska '84 failed to receive the endorsement of the Bureau of International Expositions. Fair officials were concerned that the high cost of travelling to Alaska would make "experiencing individualism" a luxury that only the affluent could afford.[13] This decision was made, of course, only after a considerable amount of money had been invested in planning the fair. An estimated $400,000 had been spent to pay salaries for Alaska '84 board mem-

13. New Orleans, with its fair theme of "The World of Rivers—Freshwater as the Source of Life," received the support of the Bureau of International Expositions.

bers, to produce a ten-minute color film promoting the fair (a mixture of nature photography and shots of "adventurous individuals"—DaVinci, Einstein, American astronauts), and to hire consultants to design the fair grounds.[14] Funding was supplied by various sources that hoped to benefit from increased tourism and capital expenditures resulting from the fair. The State of Alaska contributed $200,000, the Municipality of Anchorage $50,000, and an additional $50,000 came from private donations. The remaining $100,000 was reportedly advanced by Uchitel himself.

In retrospect, Alaska '84 might be considered a costly venture for everyone involved. Nevertheless, those interested in furthering tourism in the forty-ninth state have not given up. In a more recent move in this direction, the state has aggressively sought the bid for the 1992 Winter Olympic Games. Recognizing that the key to attracting visitors to Alaska lies in marketing the qualities of individualism and independence that are a part of its northern image, promoters of Alaskan tourism are actively engaged in producing a twentieth-century analogue to the nineteenth-century American frontier.

The Call of the Pseudo-Wild: Exporting the Frontier Myth

Travel to Alaska is still sufficiently expensive to preclude even that once-in-a-lifetime visit to the state for all but a few Americans. The vast majority must be content with the image of Alaska that is supplied by the media. Although media coverage of Alaska peaked during construction of the oil pipeline, the publishing industry has long been interested in the exotic aspects of Alaskan life. One firm that has successfully marketed Alaska to thousands of readers is

14. Sergio Bernardes, the noted Brazilian architect, was one of those who flew to Anchorage to meet with Uchitel and the Alaska '84 steering committee.

Alaska Publishing Properties. In the last half of 1985, the average circulation of *Alaska: The Magazine of Life on the Last Frontier* was over 150,000 copies per month. Although a large percentage of sales occurs within the Pacific region of the United States, the majority of readers live in other parts of the country (Audit Bureau of Circulations, 1986). The format of *Alaska* magazine is similar to that of other travel publications that feature the more interesting side of adventure states. Most of the articles are devoted to the scenic beauty and unique qualities of rural Alaska and only occasionally provide accounts of life in Anchorage or Fairbanks.

Insight into the content and effect of the Alaskan image that *Alaska* magazine presents to its readership may be found in the "Letters, Notes, and Comments" section of the magazine. In addition to responding to substantive issues raised in feature articles, many entries in this section underscore the general significance of the magazine itself.[15] Specifically, they make explicit the claim that reading *Alaska* magazine provides a meaningful alternative to visiting the frontier state. Consider the following representative examples:

> We feel as if by reading your articles and seeing your gorgeous colored photos that we have taken a trip to

15. One might raise the objection that "Letters to the Editor" features in magazines are subject to editorial selection and revision and therefore do not represent a valid source of data. To this objection, I would offer two responses. First, while in Anchorage, I visited the offices of Alaska Northwest Publishing Company (then the publisher of *Alaska* magazine) to inquire about the procedure for editorial selection. I was told that all responses to the magazine were printed, so that any possible bias in presentation was a consequence of editorial revision. Yet, even if one accepts this claim prima facie, the most compelling reasons for presenting these data lie in their support for the *image* of Alaska that a publishing company wishes to convey to its readership: that Alaska is unique when compared with the other forty-nine states and that this uniqueness can mean something to everyone. The letters appearing in the text are taken from an archival search of *Alaska* magazine covering a ten-year period (1970 to 1979).

Alaska by remote control each month. (Mrs. Carl A. Skrenes, Madison, Wisconsin)

I am an armchair dreamer of the Alaskan adventures your magazine shares with me. Like so many others, I only talk about going to Alaska. While only 29, I come closer to this dream each month when I receive your sensitive publication. (Daniel B. VanCampen, North Hollywood, California)

I recently purchased a copy of your magazine and once I thumbed through it I got the same old dream I've had for 30 years. Well, if I can't live my dream at least I can read about it. (Frank Mitchell, Harrisburg, Illinois)

Reading—and dreaming—about Alaska is one way of experiencing the frontier. Just like those of prospective migrants and visitors to Alaska, the dreams of "would-be Alaskans" are filled with images of a land where life is simpler, a place that remains untrammeled by the problems associated with industrialization and contemporary urban life.

We sure do enjoy your magazine. We call it our escape from the humdrum of city life. (Mrs. Mary Richmond, Posen, Illinois)

After a day's work in this so-called modern world with air pollution and noise, it is a real escape to sit down and read *Alaska* magazine. Let's hope there is some way to keep Alaska the way your magazine describes it, for there is very little peace and quiet and clean air left in this world today. (Roy B. Nance, Honolulu, Hawaii)

But in addition to offering a momentary escape to those who live outside the state, *Alaska* magazine goes further to suggest that Alaska may be a cure for individual ills. The implication of the following letter is that the spirit of Alaska may be realized in the "commodified" form of the travel magazine (cf. Goldman and Dickens, 1983).

Tonight I reread an extraordinary short story by Dan Strickland, and as I sit by my fire listening to piano music, I can almost see the moon lavish over the snowy landscape with its soft light and silence and can almost hear the chorus of wolves in the distant valley. Just as Mr. Strickland, I almost felt transported back to earlier times, but soon realized that Springfield is not Alaska. However, *Alaska* magazine provides a tremendous service to the lower states. For example, I keep Mr. Strickland's article and reread it when I feel down and need a lift. It gives me a fresh start and helps me gain a new perspective when things get lopsided as they often do when you are a bureaucrat. (Chet Dixon, Springfield, Missouri)

What a publication like *Alaska* magazine does, then, is to perpetuate the image of Alaska as an American frontier and to suggest that this image can mean something to everyone, not just to those living in Alaska. It seeks to have Outsiders identify with the spirit of Alaska and to let them know that there is hope for the problems of the world. It presents Alaska as a "solvegoat," where "just the idea of Alaska" is a panacea for troubled times (*Anchorage Times,* August 12, 1979). And like Bob Uchitel's Alaska '84, it holds out the forty-ninth state as an example for others to follow. Quite simply, it strives to make those who have never ventured north feel like Alaskans. As one reader put it:

The spirit of Alaska exists in the hearts of all men and women everywhere. Your magazine helps to bring this spirit to the surface. (Richard Nelson, Harborcreek, Pennsylvania)

Doug Herring and "Alaska, The Musical"

A more recent attempt at the commodification of the frontier myth came in the form of a musical that would have packaged the Alaskan image for mass consumption. Although the effort failed, it deserves mention because it illustrates an updating of the traditional image of Alaska.

"Alaska, The Musical" grew out of a reaction to what Doug Herring (a previous Alaskan) viewed as a growing attack on individual freedoms. Americans must realize, Herring and his associates insist, that their frontiers are being threatened by an increasing measure of federal intervention. To get their point across, the producers of the show printed posters and T-shirts that carried the theme of the musical: "Alaska—Land of the Individual and Other Endangered Species." The way in which Alaskans lead the rest of the nation away from governmental control provides the plot for "Alaska, The Musical" (Herring, 1978).

The play opens at the turn of the next century when people are "true individuals" once again. The audience is then transported back to the 1960s and 1970s to find a group of discontented Alaskans who are concerned with saving the "adventuresome lifestyle" of their state. Realizing the growing pressures of a "runaway" federal government, they decide to fight back. They hit upon the idea of expressing their message through entertainment and form a travelling show. As fate would have it, they encounter opposition from federal agents bent on sabotaging their mission. But the agents are overwhelmed by the "lightheartedness and unbridled determination" of the musical Alaskans, who, as we might expect, have the last word.

The statement that "Alaska, The Musical" makes is that a successful future rests in preserving the spirit of individualism. If Alaskans are the ones to lead us in that direction, it is because their state symbolizes that esteemed American trait. One of the producers of the musical comments: "There are a lot of Alaskans who haven't arrived here yet. *The Alaskan spirit is a commodity that Alaskans can export—an attitude.* Not everyone can handle the climate, but they can handle the attitude. There is a bit of Alaskan in everybody" (emphasis mine). The case could not be more clearly stated. The frontier aspects of Alaska are available to those who would find it difficult to live in a more primitive setting. And although the landscape of the Alaskan frontier has changed, it is doubtful whether the image of that landscape has been affected to the same degree.

Conclusion

Because the image of Alaska is a marketable commodity, it has been transported to places outside of the state. Those who wish to promote an interest an Alaska among potential migrants, visitors, and other Outsiders endeavor to keep alive the pioneer images associated with the forty-ninth state. To the extent they are successful, Alaska holds an attraction analogous to that of the American West, what one frontier historian referred to as a "socio-psychological safety valve":

> Even those American workers who would never be able to escape to the frontier were willing to endure their plight because they *believed* that one day they would. This belief rested on some foundation, for the sequential development of successive Wests created an opportunity for upward social mobility unparalleled in other nations. . . . The frontier did offer solace to the oppressed by conjuring visions of limitless opportunity amid virgin wealth of the West, and even though few found the pot of gold, the faith that it could be found persisted. Not every gambler must win to keep the faith in gamblers alive. (Billington, 1974:37–38)

The history of America is largely a history of frontiers, for when one region faded from the limelight, another came to the fore. As gold was running out in one part of the country, a bigger lode was being discovered in another. And in the twentieth century, while there is much discussion of business, scientific, and extra-terrestrial frontiers, some will continue to view Alaska as the last American, landed frontier. "The world needs an embodiment of the frontier mythology, the sense of horizons unexplored, the mystery of uninhabited miles. It needs a place where the wolves stalk the stand lines in the dark, because a land that can produce a wolf is a healthy, robust, and perfect land" (Weeden, 1973).

Alaska *is* that myth made reality for many Americans. That is why some insist that many "Alaskans" live outside the forty-ninth state and why the frontier image of Alaska will survive the changes in landscape that the state will experience in the future.

CHAPTER 6

A Sense of Place

This analysis of the Alaskan frontier may be read as a case study of a small number of Americans who view themselves as contemporary pioneers. Their quest for a unique way of life continues a traditional American preoccupation with frontiers, and the experiences they create and share are shaped by the antecedents of that tradition. More broadly, however, their story raises fundamental questions about what frontiers and communities as places mean to people and about how collective identities can arise in response to place.

In this final chapter I look beyond the Alaskan frontier to examine the usefulness of "frontier" and "community" as fundamental concepts of the social sciences today. I will argue that they remain powerful symbols of American culture and that the conditions of modern life—in particular, urbanization, population mobility, and heterogeneity—have played a major role in sustaining their importance. The closing of the frontier and the loss of community, both of which were mourned near the beginning of this century, did more to elevate these symbols in the hierarchy of cultural values than to diminish them. It was not until they had ceased to occupy a particular physical form that the importance of frontier and community could be fully realized.

Frontier Reconsidered

Although historians have been the principal guardians of scholarly frontier lore, they have been joined by students of economics, politics, and community life in their exploration of frontiers. How they approached the topic reflected the larger concerns of their respective disciplines. Economists described the patterns of resource dominance and exploita- tion that characterized the relationship between established regions and outlying territories. Political scientists reviewed the role of colonialism in relation to national expansion. And sociologists, prompted by an interest in the newness of life on the frontier, focused on the processes of community creation and development. Although each of these excur- sions represented a broadening of disciplinary scope, none of them challenged the original conceptualizations of frontier posited by historians. In short, they relied upon historians to identify, in space and in time, the location of their units of analysis. It was not so much the task of the economist, political scientist, and sociologist to *find* frontiers as it was theirs to describe and analyze the frontiers discovered by historians.

Such analytic strategies carry with them significant im- plications. In the absence of a reconceptualization of frontier, scholarly work has proceeded in one of two diver- gent directions. Either we have assumed that our audiences would know what was meant by frontier, so that it was, in effect, left undefined, or we have followed the path cleared by Turner—that of attaching many definitions to the con- cept—leaving, as a result, frontier without definitional con- sensus.

This conceptual vagueness is exacerbated by the popularity that the frontier has sustained in the public mind. Because the concept is woven into the fabric of American culture in so many different ways, analytic dissection of "frontier" is complicated by the myriad of evaluative components that have been attached to a single term. I hope to add a measure of conceptual clarity to an already cloudy debate. My goal is not to offer a particular definition as superior to others, but rather to outline the facets that these many definitions of frontier share. In doing so, the similarities between frontier and other well-established concepts in the sociologi- cal literature should become apparent.

Two structural properties give rise to the distinct features we have often confused with the frontier itself. These are the specification of a frontier in terms of its *relation* to some larger whole and its *distant position* from the center of that whole. Although both of these characteristics appear to be obvious criteria for any frontier, they have been accorded surprisingly little attention by frontier scholars. Yet it is from these basic components that the peculiarities of frontiers flow.

By the first quality, the relational nature of frontier, I mean that a frontier must always be thought of as a component of some larger whole, and, as a part of that whole, must be defined in relation to another part. To describe something as a frontier requires that one simultaneously provide an answer to the question: "A frontier *of what*" (cf. Hayes, 1946)? There is, of course, considerable variation in what one considers the whole to be—an academic discipline or all of knowledge itself, a nation-state or the world—and the designation of this larger whole constrains the specification of an appropriate frontier. In this sense the whole imparts meaning to its constituent parts.

On the other hand, the second element of frontier—its distant position from the core of some whole—imparts a certain unity to the whole by defining its limits. This positional element of the concept means that a frontier is the part *farthest removed* from the center of the whole. Just as the specification of whole and part is marked by immense latitude, so too are the criteria by which distance is measured between core and frontier. Because of the frontier's close association with military conquest and territorial expansion throughout history, we have commonly described frontiers in terms of their geographic distance from settlements of greater density. But in recent years frontiers have been placed in an ever-increasing variety of settings—at the edges of institutional forms, social values, even time (Melbin, 1978)—all of which have little to do with location in physical space.

No matter how great the distance separating frontier from center, the two are bound up in a single whole and derive their place in that whole through reflexive definition. Any frontier has as its point of reference some center, and any core derives its sense of centrality through comparison with its frontier. Once this reciprocity ceases, the part that once marked the edge of the whole moves *outside* of it and, correspondingly, changes status from frontier to "counter-core."

Defined in terms of these structural properties, frontiers are essentially similar in their conceptual elements to a number of other concepts in the literature of sociology. In several important respects the concepts of core and frontier sketched here correspond to Edward Shils's (1975) analysis of the central institutional and value systems of society. In his essays on macrosociology, he writes:

> Every society . . . may be interpreted as a center and a periphery. The center consists of those institutions (and roles) which exercise authority—whether it be economic, governmental, political, military—and of those which create and diffuse cultural symbols—religious, literary, etc. The periphery consists of those strata or sectors of the society which are the recipients of commands and of beliefs which they do not themselves create or cause to be diffused, and of those who are lower in the distribution or allocation of rewards, dignities, facilities, etc. (Shils, 1975:39)

Within this conceptual framework, then, the frontier is analogous to that segment of a society that is least powerful, least rewarded, least affected by the cultural or institutional system that emanates from the center. The greater the distance between center and periphery, the more tenuous their association.[1]

1. In world-system theory, the concepts of core, periphery, and semi-periphery also play a major role in analyses of economic development in the Third World (Wallerstein, 1974; 1980).

A similar focus on reciprocal relations is explicit in Georg Simmel's (1950) work on the role of the "stranger" in group life. As an element of the group itself, the stranger occupies a position that is, at once, "near and far" to other group members; through the coordinated and constant interaction of group members, the role of stranger is stabilized, thereby becoming a fixed element of the group. Rather than a sporadic participant in group life, the stranger is one who "comes today and stays tomorrow."

Although the conceptual linkages are less direct than in the former two, Robert Park's (1928) discussion of the "marginal man" is also relevant here. Rather than on the edges of a single whole, the marginal man occupies "the margin of two cultures and two societies, which never completely interpenetrated and fused." Park attributes the rise of the marginal man to increased cultural contact brought on by massive migration but notes that such factors coalesce in a personality type characterized by a relatively permanent "period of crisis." The central problem facing the marginl man, then, is coping with the tension that arises where the margins of two cultures intersect.

Each of these conceptual schema—"center/periphery," "stranger," and "marginal man"—share the explicit criteria that I have attributed to frontiers, a distant, yet unified relationship to some core. Yet there is an additional element implicit in these other concepts that frontier does not share. This characteristic is primarily concerned with the evaluative imagery with which the periphery, stranger, and marginal man are cloaked. Assuming the perspective of the center as the embodiment of the socially or culturally essential, a move away from that center signals a shift to a less important position in the social or cultural order. It follows from such a viewpoint that the fundamental, representative elements of a whole—and therefore those that are most socially or culturally valued—will be found at the center of that whole, not at its edges.

This sense of social or cultural devaluation of peripheral parts is absent from the imagery surrounding descriptions of contemporary frontiers. Clearly, such was not always the case; throughout most of history, landed frontiers were depicted in terms of their inferiority to the established centers of cultural and social life (Juricek, 1960). Over time, however, observers of nineteenth-century America gradually came to see their frontiers in a favorable light, and the frontier thesis of Turner did not so much introduce a completely new view of frontier life as it did crystallize an image that was emerging at that time. It was Turner who argued that the peripheral regions of the country were no less "American" than its core. On the contrary, he insisted that the frontier was the *source* of the American character itself and the pioneer the paragon of all American virtues. In doing so, he broke ground for those who would incorporate the frontier as a metaphor for progress into many spheres transcending physical space.

Turner, and others like him who sought to document the critical importance of the frontier to the nation, faced serious scholarly challenges regarding the historical validity of their argument, but they found in the American public an audience eager to embrace the frontier as its dominant cultural image. Not only was the frontier adopted as the tangible sign of national progress but, more important, it stood as the *symbolic representation* of limitless opportunity—a social-psychological safety valve—for those who would never venture west. Although the acceptance of frontier in this manner no doubt enhanced the lives of those at the nation's center, it simultaneously endowed the American frontier with a vital resource—the power to shape the imagery of the national character. If we conceive of the core of the nation as harboring a preponderance of political and economic resources, then we may view the frontier as the repository of valued cultural symbols. Today many Americans look to Alaska as the place where those images abound.

This conceptualization of the relationship between core and frontier in terms of the control and exchange of resources (both real and symbolic) modifies a research tradition that has focused on the asymmetrical exploitation of frontier by core. Frontiers have often been portrayed as lands of plenty, rich in resources necessary to fuel an aging and declining society. In contrast, I am suggesting that where frontier is recognized as a valued symbolic resource it may be used to support the exploitation of core by frontier. If this is true, then we would expect the Alaskan frontier to attempt to maintain control over its symbolic resources in the same way that a core would be expected to seek a greater concentration of state power.

How a frontier retains its monopoly of frontier imagery is closely tied to the relationship linking frontier and core. Because frontier and core are parts of a unitary whole, their relational status provides the impetus for group differentiation and identification. By comparing themselves with those at the center of the nation, those on the Alaskan frontier define a separate and unique place for themselves within the nation as a whole. As my analysis in Chapter 3 demonstrates, residents of Anchorage think of Alaskans as characteristically different and, in a sense, "more American" than other Americans. Concern for their role within a larger system is also a major source of group identity for Alaskan residents, for in coming to see themselves as different from others, they construct the foundation of their similarities. The distinctions Anchorage residents draw between "Outsiders" and Alaskans are powerful factors in the creation of community in Alaska.

Furthermore, because the relationship between frontier and core is a distant one, it is likely that those at the core and those on the frontier will have limited contact; in the absence of direct experience, these two groups will act toward one another on the basis of limited information and stereotypes (Brewer and Campbell, 1976; LeVine and Campbell, 1972). The geographic location of the Alaskan frontier enhances the processes of group differentiation and identification. Assuming the perspective of the frontier, this means that projection of a valued cultural image is largely a matter of information control. Because few Americans will have had direct contact with the Alaskan frontier, those living in Alaska may supply information to others that will bolster their claim to cultural singularity. If such attempts prove successful, the collective identity of Alaskans is reinforced to the extent that, should they come into contact with Outsiders, they will be expected to display signs of their uniqueness.[2]

The same factors that sustain the frontier as a cultural symbol, however, create the central tensions that dominate the relations between Alaska and the rest of the country. Insofar as distance and interconnectedness give rise to the singularity of the frontier, they also reinforce the economic and political dominance of the core. To draw a frontier closer to the center is to destroy its uniqueness, and failure to demonstrate the essential ties between center and periphery is to provide the core with ideological support for devaluation and exploitation of the frontier. As Alaskans pondered the political, economic, and social ties of Alaska to the other states through the workings of the Alaska Statehood Commission, they were constantly reminded of the precariousness that accompanies such public displays of "marginal differentiation" (Reisman, 1954). For as they attempt to project an image of Alaskans as different but not *too* different from other Americans, they must be sensitive to their own desire for a valued collective identity, while anticipating how others are likely to see them.

The process of marginal differentiation is fraught with complexities in times when core and periphery exist in close proximity to one another, when great numbers of a society

2. These generalities are necessarily phrased in probabilistic terms, as it is open to question whether location in social or physical space is followed by the particular response outlined above. A similar concern engendered a lengthy exchange among theorists who challenged the notion that a "marginal status" would be manifested in the social-psychological form of a "marginal personality" (McLemore, 1970; Kerchoff and McCormick, 1955). Here, I have posited a frontier that is relatively distinct and distant from its core. In cases in which these conditions are not met, one would expect support for these hypotheses to be correspondingly weaker.

interact with and are attached to the center. Yet the need to mark differences in this largely undifferentiated "mass society" (as Shils used the term) is, at the same time, all the more pressing. This is exactly the task facing residents of Anchorage, Alaska, in the latter half of the twentieth century: to define the role of the frontier in contemporary American society.

Community Reconsidered

As I have noted at various times throughout this book, intertwined with the concept of frontier is that of community. Here, I will use the illustration of the Alaskan frontier to discuss the general relevance of community as place in the modern world. An integral part of who Alaskans are is derived from where they live, a fact that draws attention to the role of place in defining community: how place has been incorporated as a dimension of community in the past and how it continues to provide the context for community today.

Addressing these concerns requires trodding over some familiar, yet fertile, theoretical ground. What do places mean to people? How do people attach themselves to places? Of what significance is place to the creation of community? Classical approaches to the study of community have provided remarkably consistent answers to these questions. They have argued that as the scope of interaction reached across local boundaries, the importance of place in community and identity declined. Once a taken-for-granted aspect of community, the role of place in defining identity and community in modern life has become problematic. Yet this study of Anchorage, Alaska, suggests that place remains a viable source of community, although in a different analytic sense than it has been used in the past. After providing a context for this conclusion through a review of the concept of community, I will discuss the contemporary

Alaskan frontier as an example of how modern life has created, rather than undermined, the conditions for community as place. And finally, in looking beyond the case of Alaska, I will suggest a broader search for "communities of place" in the modern world.

The Loss of Community

The many classic typologies constructed by students of community offered similar descriptions of two contrasting ways of life. *Community* represented the natural, almost instinctual aspects of human association: ties of blood and locality. Relationships were governed by a high degree of intimacy and contact, and sentiments of group membership overshadowed any sense of self apart from others. As a product of tradition, communal life celebrated stability and eschewed change. *Society,* by contrast, was a human creation held together by tenuous bonds of self-interest. Interaction was premised on a distinction between means and ends and fragmented by a multiplicity of institutional roles. In every way community was portrayed as the mirror opposite of society.

In addition, these dichotomies relied on the same historical imperative—the progresive replacement of community with society. Indeed, the proliferation of modern, secondary associations was thought to decrease the opportunity for communal associations (Gusfield, 1975). The face-to-face gave way to the anonymous, the natural to the artificial, and the stable to an era of constant change. Community and society came to be viewed as competing ways of life present in zero-sum quantities.

The decline of community was not only noted; its passing was mourned. Along with their use as analytic concepts of social science, community and society came laden with evaluative imagery. It was not just that one way of life had superseded the other; the often explicit message was that modern society was less meaningful, less satisfying, and altogether less desirable than traditional life. In the United States, the diminution of small-town agricultural settlements was often associated with this theme of "lost community." Responding to dramatic changes in the social landscape of the country, Jefferson, Emerson, Thoreau, and others focused their attacks on American cities, adding strength to a profound national tradition of anti-urbanism. The cherished traits associated with rural, frontier life—courage, determinism, self-sufficiency, honesty, resourcefulness, friendliness, hard work—defined the essential elements of what was American. Without them, the vitality of national institutions was threatened. The frustration associated with attempts to recapture these virtues was apparent in Turner's grim pronouncement that "the free lands that made the American pioneer have gone." What was at stake with the loss of community (and the loss of "free land"), then, was the national identity—an assault on the American character. In many quarters, the growth of cities appeared to undermine the symbol of community as metaphor for the national ideal.

The effects of this loss of community, nonetheless, extended beyond their symbolic importance. As the nation became more urbanized, the study of society focused on every aspect of city life. No social institution was found to be immune to the effects of urbanism. Factors of population size, density, and heterogeneity created transient and superficial forms of human association. The ecological forces that propelled urban growth were invested with a life of their own, destroying traditional forms of community in their wake. According to early sociologists, most notably those of the Chicago School, the city became a breeding ground of social disorganization.

By mid-century, the initial fear that American cities would eliminate any vestiges of communal life was dissipated by an expanding collection of urban ethnographies. Whyte's *Street Corner Society* (1943), Jacobs' *The Death and Life of Great American Cities* (1961), Gans's *The Urban Villagers* (1962), Liebow's *Tally's Corner* (1967)—these and many other portraits of urban life revealed that islands of traditional life survived in the midst of large urban centers and that the growth of cities did not inevitably promote a corresponding decrease in forms of traditional communal association. Some urban residents retained close friendships, felt strong ties to the neighborhood in which they lived, and clung to traditional values and beliefs. These "urban villagers" spent significant portions of their lives buffered from the turbulent currents of urban life within the boundaries of community. Although these ethnographic portraits depicted the city as a puzzle of various socially organized pieces (instead of a system tending toward *disorganization*), they too identified an element of conflict between traditional and modern life. Community persisted *despite* urban change because it was impervious to its deleterious effects. The traditional and the modern coexisted but, to borrow from the Chicago sociologists, they did not "interpenetrate."

Community Transformed:
The Creation of Community from Society

The perspective of the urban village introduced a significant challenge to the empirical incompatibility of community and society. Of greater significance, however, are recent challenges to the *conceptual* incompatibility between the ways of life represented by these concepts. Rather than analytic opposites, community and society have been redefined as complementary elements engaged in a dialectic generating new forms of collective life. Claude Fischer (1975), for example, has argued not only that cities harbor community, but also that they in fact *create* the conditions for community by fostering the development of viable subcultures. Social groups are strengthened, not destroyed, in the face of increasing urbanization in two ways. First, through the attraction of sufficiently large numbers of migrants, cities establish a critical mass of potential subculture members. As population increases, so does the likelihood that those sharing specific interests will find opportunities for intensive interaction. Second, cities provide a setting that encourages intergroup contact. As the home of heterogeneous social worlds, urban areas promote opportunities for displays of group differences. In responding to these differences, members of subcultures may cling more firmly to their particular social worlds (Fischer, 1975).

Fischer's "subcultural theory" is intriguing because it imparts new meaning to the connection between structural elements of urban growth and the generation of social worlds posited in the theories of the Chicago sociologists. Although these earlier theorists viewed the city as the home of numerous "natural areas," they did not consider these to be representative of communal forms of association. Fischer's primary contribution is to modify this perspective by suggesting that although cities do not foster the conditions that replicate traditional communal life, they do allow for the creation of community in distinctly modern forms. Heterogeneity and density of urban populations thus increase the opportunities for recognizing group differences. In Fischer's analysis, the result is the creation of community within subcultures characterized by diversity of race, ethnicity, sexual preference, political orientation, or class affiliation.

In their most general form, reassessments of urban life such as Fischer's reveal how the social relations associated with traditional forms of community develop from a multiplicity of sources. More important, they focus attention on the ways in which modern urban life shapes the meaning and form of contemporary communal experience. Urban growth does not destroy community; it gives life to it.

In line with this perspective, my analysis of contemporary Alaska demonstrates how both the meaning and the structure of community have been created and, in the process, transformed by modern society. By its use as a counter-concept to community, society establishes the cultural standard against which the image of community is formed. Community could not be appreciated until the nation had become sufficiently urbanized and, in that sense, had to be "lost" before it could achieve its status as a metaphor for the "good life." In a similar manner, the American frontier could achieve a prominent place as a cultural symbol only *after* the taming of the wild. Had the Bureau of the Census not declared the frontier "closed" near the beginning of this century, Turner's glorification of the American pioneer could not have received the same attention. The reflexive definition of frontier and core—or rural and urban—is dependent on stark conceptual contrast.

In Alaska, nowhere is this contrast more striking than in Anchorage. Anchorage appears to be everything that a frontier is not: densely populated compared with the rest of Alaska, economically propelled by occupations that are far removed from the land, and protected from the inconveniences of nature by an inexhaustive availability of urban amenities. But rather than destroy the basis for identification with Alaska as a frontier, urbanization in Alaska has shaped the meaning of a contemporary frontier way of life. Without an Anchorage, one could reasonably argue that the search for a modern-day frontier would prove even more elusive.

Because their city is emblematic of what many consider to be the least "Alaskan" part of Alaska, Anchorage residents are forced into a more extensive search for identification with the Alaskan frontier image. In fact, the content of their place identities as "Alaskans" is formed largely in response to the urban (and, therefore, "non-Alaskan") aspects of life in Anchorage. In much the same way that Anchorage acts as a magnet attracting economic and political resources from throughout the state, it draws on the more primitive aspects of Alaskan frontier life to construct its image as a pioneer outpost. This is clearly illustrated in the nominal identification of Anchorage residents. They derive their sense of place through association with the state as a whole—as "Alaskans"—rather than with smaller territorial units, such as block, neighborhood, or even local community. The series of reorientations of language, space, and time described in

Chapter 4 acts to attach Anchorage residents to the larger image of the Alaskan frontier. By framing their experiences in these terms, Anchorage residents are united by a common history that serves as a basis for community. Just as a particular communal identity can arise in response to the idea of modern society, the structural characteristics of urban life may affect how a sense of community is acquired. Given the prevalence of geographic mobility in modern life, one would hardly expect birthright to be the major criterion on which ties to local community are premised. A sense of place more likely evolves out of a process of achievement, a dynamic that depends as much on the actions of others as on those of oneself. Urban life engages this dynamic by generating opportunities for comparisons. Caught up in the forces of population mobility and heterogeneous interaction, urban residents are placed in the position of reflecting on their similarities, which, in turn, may serve as the basis for communal solidarity.

For Fischer (1975), two structural properties of modern life—population size and heterogeneity—create community in the form of a world of urban subcultures. For Anchorage residents, a third ecological process—migration—is a critical factor in the creation of communal identity.[3] Ironically, rather than diminish the role of place in the formation of community and identity, geographic mobility *intensifies* identification with place. Mobility, and the concomitant opportunities it brings for interaction and comparison, provides the context for how residents themselves acquire and how others attribute to them an identity as Alaskans.

The process of Alaskan migration reinforces the characterization of Alaska as a frontier. Prior to moving, images of a wild and exotic Alaska color the expectations of Anchorage migrants and figure prominently into their deci-

---

3. The process of migration is also important to Fischer's subcultural theory to the extent that it is responsible for the formation of a "critical mass" of subculture members. It is not, however, the principal factor responsible for the generation of communal identity as I suggest here.

sions to move. This picture of Alaska is simultaneously affirmed by the response of friends and relatives of potential migrants. The mention of moving to Alaska is apt to generate animated discussion about "the kind of person who moves there." Indeed, as this study has shown, some newcomers to Anchorage will have already identified themselves as different from others—perhaps more adventurous or more independent—before they arrive.

Once the migrants arrive, the comparisons generated by moving to Alaska continue to foster a unique sense of place among Anchorage residents. As they come to see themselves as Alaskans, they do so within the context of biographies that have been constructed outside of Alaska. By using that other life as a point of reference, Anchorage residents define the elements of their current experience that distinguish Alaska from other places. The Alaska they create is one based on comparatives: its people friendlier and more independent; its economic opportunities greater and more challenging; its government more accessible and the results of government more immediately felt. These comparatives, in turn, form the basis of ties among Anchorage residents as a community of migrants.

The distinctiveness of Alaskan life is shored up through interaction with non-residents. When Anchorage residents return to the continental United States, not only their friends and family members, but strangers as well, expect them to display visible signs of their Alaskan experiences. These encounters shed light on the acquisition of place identity in that some residents begin to think of themselves as Alaskans only after they travel outside of the state. Thus, at least in part, residents of Anchorage assume a frontier mien because it is expected of them.[4]

4. Many have noted the effect of definitions of others on the formation of group identity. Shibutani and Kwan (1965:210) note that "those who are treated alike gradually come to conceive of themselves in the same manner." Giddings (1922) referred to a similar phenomenon as a "consciousness of kind," and more recently, Hunter (1974) describes the "looking glass community" in his study of Chicago neighborhoods.

In addition to these micro-level responses that encourage attachment to Alaska, the fact that Anchorage is the site of rapid population turnover also promotes place identity. High rates of in- and out-migration provide a constant supply of newcomers, who then serve as a reference group for others already living in Anchorage. In comparing themselves with these new arrivals, residents of only short duration come to think of themselves as seasoned veterans of Alaska. Their claim to community membership in adopting the "Alaskan" label rests on the repeated turnover of the Anchorage population.[5]

The process of migration is thus crucial to the development of community and identity in Anchorage in two ways. As a social-psychological factor, it forms the basis for comparing Alaska with other places in the country, and as an ecological factor, it establishes standards of community membership within Anchorage as a community of migrants. This relationship between migration and community identity constitutes one of the central ironies of Alaskan life. The tenuous but recent ties of Alaskan migrants to place would appear antithetical to the development of strong attachments to local community. Yet these are the very qualities that promote and enhance identification with place.

These counterintuitive findings from Alaska raise larger questions about "communities of place" in modern life. In a world of frequent residential mobility, widely dispersed net-

5. The effects of mobility on place identities are, of course, not unique to Alaska. Although the content of the Alaskan identity is derived from a particular historical tradition, an analogous process through which place identities are acquired should be found elsewhere. For example, one would expect residents of communities that witness similar patterns of migration to begin to identify with their new location more quickly than migrants to communities that harbor largely stable populations. Identification with place may thus assume a similar pattern in cities such as Atlanta and Houston that serve as collecting points for "chronic movers" (Morrison, 1971), a group accounting for a disproportionate share of internal migration.

works of interaction, and permeable community boundaries, can place provide a meaningful context for community?

Communities of Place:
Place as Territory and Symbol in Community Life

Of the many characteristics of community, one of the most frequently employed is place as shared territory. This is not surprising in light of the intellectual tradition from which the study of community arose. A not insignificant part of the historical shift from community to society concerned the changing role of place in the modern world. In community, attachment to place was total and automatic. Here was a world of little geographic or social mobility, where no sense of self could exist apart from a sense of place. In our histories, we know the inhabitants of these times from their place names—Francis of Assisi, John of Gaunt, Joan of Arc. To be separated from locality meant to lose one's place— literally—in the world, not only in one's own eyes but in the eyes of others.

This view of history carried over to community research, where territorial aspects of community formed an essential part of representations of communcal life (Hillary, 1955; Effrat, 1974). Community studies initially focused on territory as at once an impetus to and a constraint on interaction. Physical proximity provided the context for face-to-face interaction, which, in turn, served as the foundation for community institutions. But at the same time that location made interaction possible, it limited it. In interacting with one set of actors, one was precluded from interacting with others.

Along with changes in technology, modern life brought alternatives for interaction. In earlier times when social and geographic location were coterminous, the significance of the relationship between the two could not be assessed. But as communication and transportation expanded the range of possible interaction across time and space, new perspectives of community arose that challenged the role of territory in community building. In a world of easily separable and frequently separated ties to locality, shared territory was thought to be of relatively minor importance in the construction of communal identity. In the modern world, it was possible to have "community without propinquity" (Webber, 1963) or to delineate networks that linked urban residents in a complex system of affiliations based on friendship, occupational, recreational, or other ties (e.g., a "community of scholars"). Freed of territorial constraints, community became a product of self-conscious and purposive action, yet one that was thought to provide the same functions—such as assistance and solidarity—as those attributed to communities grounded in locality (Wellman, 1979).

Neither of these conceptual traditions—"community of place" or "community without place"—accord territory a significant, *independent* role in the generation of community. This is obviously true of those advocating community without place, where locality is altogether ignored in defining community. But even when posited as a criterion for community by those defending the community of place, territory is important only insofar as it is a necessary precondition for other, social aspects of community—intense interaction and institutional development. Place, in that sense, was important to descriptions of community primarily because interaction had to occur somewhere.

More important, by not according place an independent role in the development of community, we ignore more than real estate. People have long recognized that place was more than mere physical territory, that places are repositories of images that shape expectations and guide behavior. But the symbolic aspects of place have, by and large, not been given sufficient attention by students of community. By neglecting the symbolic importance of place in community, we have failed to appreciate how the context of community life remains vital to its content.

Places are known in a variety of ways—by their climates, their histories, their ecologies, and the ways of life they support. There are neighborhoods where we feel safe, others where we do not; cities like Boston and Philadelphia that are indelibly marked by historical events; and others like Los Angeles and Anchorage that seem totally modern and devoid of any sense of tradition. Depending upon our purpose, we may seek out one type of place rather than another, often acting on the basis of place imagery. In fact, in the absence of direct experience with a place, our sense of place may be wholly constituted by these images.

As elements of culture, images of places are not the product of individual action and, therefore, cannot be made or unmade at will. But this does not mean that they are immutable. As blacks move into a previously all-white neighborhood, for example, or as young professionals alter the physical and social landscape of an inner-city neighborhood through gentrification, conceptions change as to what constitutes a desirable place to live. When conflict arises as a result of these transitions, the debate centers not just on property values and city services, but also on what kind of place residents consider their neighborhood to be.

Although we have identified social processes that transcend place boundaries, the context of community interaction is always particular and specific. When residents discuss what goes on in their communities, they are not talking about cocktail parties, barking dogs, friendly neighbors, ill-kept houses, as abstract, physical realities; rather, they are talking about "his" dog, "that nice, new couple," or "their" house. Because every place constitutes a unique setting for interaction, the study of community must be particularistic in some respects.

The interpretations we impose on the happenings of everyday life give meaning to community. As community residents recognize and respond to territory and other physical aspects of place in terms of their symbolic attributes, they define standards of community membership about the kind of person who "belongs here." To the extent that community residents identify themselves as "belonging" (or others as "not belonging") to the community in these terms, a particular image of place is reinforced. The meaning of place is thus derived through everyday, local interaction; its content cannot be separated from its location.

This study of Anchorage shows that symbols of place have some basis in geographic area, no matter how broadly defined. Residents of Anchorage can claim the status of contemporary American pioneer only because they live in Alaska, and for that reason alone, living in Anchorage is not the same as living in another community. In short, the content of the Alaskan place identity is anchored in the particulars of place.

Rethinking the role of place in community requires that we consider the context as well as the process of interaction, not only that we search for the universals that govern the acquisition of identity and community in society but also that we pay attention to what is being acquired. Community arises out of the immediacy of local experience, and to focus exclusively on community as a process of interaction is to lose sight of the importance of where that interaction occurs. The places in which we live out our lives are rich in symbolic variation, and the search for community in modern life will continue to underscore this fact. Our studies of modern forms of community should reflect a concern for the images of place as well.

Research Methodology

After an initial site visit to Alaska in August and September of 1978, the majority of the fieldwork for this community study of Anchorage was completed from May to December, 1979. A return visit for the purpose of follow-up interviewing and archival data collection was made in June and July, 1983. Data for this book are drawn from a variety of sources: numerous media reports (newspaper and magazine articles, radio and television programs); interviews with selected community members (government and corporate officials, journalists, academics); attendance at public functions; and the results of an interview schedule administered to 134 Anchorage residents. The bulk of the arguments advanced here is supported by analysis of the survey data. Unless otherwise noted, all statements cited in the text were made by respondents included in the Anchorage survey.

The interview schedule (reproduced in Appendix II) was divided into four principal sections. It began by reviewing major events and expectations of respondents prior to moving to Alaska. This section included questions exploring the migration experiences of Anchorage residents: occupation and residence histories, expectations of life in Anchorage, sources of information about Alaska, previous contact (through residents or visitors) with the state, and reasons for moving to Alaska. The second part of the interview focused on a wide variety of Alaskan experiences: principal likes and dislikes about living in Alaska, leisure activities, location of close friends, frequency of contact with those outside of Alaska, factors affecting identification with Alaska, and reasons for and anticipated length of stay in the state. The third section contained a number of statements asking respondents to compare Alaskans with other Americans.[1] The interview schedule concluded with a request for standard social characteristics (e.g., income, education, race, sex, occupation). An average interview could be completed in about one hour.

Because Anchorage (and all of Alaska, for that matter) witnesses rapid population turnover, the usual difficulties associated with sample selection were exacerbated. Typical sampling frames, such as city directories and voter registration lists, are likely to be out of date at the time of publication. A systematic cluster sample drawn from maps obtained from the Anchorage Planning Department proved to be the most fruitful method of selecting respondents. The sample was composed of dwelling units selected by the following procedure.

The Municipal Tax Assessor's Office divides Anchorage into "books" and "pages." Each "book" corresponds to a grid subdivision of the community and each "page" to a subunit of this larger area. Considering each "page" as a cluster, fifty clusters were systematically selected beginning with a random start. Clusters were then located on planning department maps of housing units and, again beginning with a random start, four dwelling units per cluster were selected. This yielded a total sample size of 200 units. Because clusters were roughly equal in number of dwelling units, probability-proportionate-to-size sampling was not employed. The sample was selected in about three days.

This approach to sample selection provided a number of advantages. First, it was economical; time and budgetary constraints of the research prohibited use of an alternative random sampling technique. Second, it afforded an up-to-date method for selecting respondents. The Planning Department maps had been recently revised and reflected new housing construction in the south Anchorage area. Third, this cluster design produced variation among the types of

1. The details of the method employed in administering this section of the interview are discussed in Chapter 3.

dwelling units (trailers, apartments, and houses) and respondents (in terms of group characteristics, such as age, education, and occupation) selected. The fifty clusters represented all major residential sections of the community. A comparison of selected group characteristics of the sample with those recorded in the 1980 census reveals few major discrepancies.[2] (See Table A.1.)

From the 184 housing units containing potential respondents, 134 interviews were completed, resulting in a response rate of approximately 73 percent. A detailed summary of the response and non-response categories is shown in Table A.2. Most interviews were completed between 5 and 10 P.M. on weekdays. A number of factors account for refusals to be interviewed: satiation with surveys from governmental and private agencies; concern for personal safety (e.g., situations in which a woman appeared to be home alone); suspicion as to my real purpose in attempting to gain entry. No systematic bias appeared to be introduced into the analysis by the omission of these respondents.

When no one was present at the time of first contact, up to four return visits were made (at various times of the day) to complete the interview.[3] When I was unable to locate a dwelling unit, the most frequent problem was a "lack of fit" between the Planning Department maps and the layout of newly developed areas of Anchorage. Streets were sometimes unmarked (or unnamed) in the southern sections of the municipality, and as a result, locating housing units through reference to lot lines on maps proved impossible.

2. The two noteworthy exceptions, sex and age, are both artifacts of the interviewing process. In cases in which a dwelling unit was occupied by a cohabiting couple, the interview schedule was administered alternately to males and females. This was done to insure that sex could be used as an exogeneous variable in the analysis. The exclusion of minors from the survey accounts for the age discrepancy.

3. The method of sample selection precluded notifying potential respondents in advance. Housing units were selected on the basis of lot lines drawn on planning maps; consequently, names and addresses of respondents were not produced by this sampling process.

Table A.1. Characteristics of the 1979 Anchorage Sample and a Comparison with Those of the 1980 U.S. Census, Anchorage and Alaska

| | | | U.S. Census* | | | |
| | Sample | | Anchorage | | Alaska | |
Characteristic	Percent	Number	Percent	Number	Percent	Number
Sex:						
Male	64		52		53	
Female	36		48		47	
Total	100	(134)	100	(174,431)	100	(401,851)
Race:						
White	95		85		77	
Black	4		5		3	
Native	2		5		16	
Other	0		4		4	
Total	101	(134)	99	(174,431)	100	(401,851)
Age:						
0–14	0		26		27	
15–24	16		21		20	
25–29	17		13		12	
30–34	13		11		11	
35–44	31		14		13	
45 and over	22		16		17	
Total	99	(134)	101	(174,431)	100	(401,851)
Mean	36		N/A**		N/A	
Median	35		26		23	
Marital Status:						
Married	72		59		58	
Divorced	10		10		9	
Separated	3		2		2	
Widowed	3		2		3	
Never married	13		28		29	
Total	101	(134)	101	(128,916)†	101	(293,577)†
Education:						
Less than high school diploma	8		11		18	

Table A.1, cont.

| | Sample | | U.S. Census* | | | |
| | | | Anchorage | | Alaska | |
Characteristic	Percent	Number	Percent	Number	Percent	Number
High school						
diploma	31		40		39	
Some college	31		25		23	
College degree						
or more	31		24		21	
Total	101	(134)	100	(90,606)‡	101	(211,397)‡
Mean	14.2 years		N/A		N/A	
Median	13.9 years		13.0 years		12.8 years	
Occupation:						
Managerial,						
professional	22		31		29	
Technical, ad-						
ministrative						
support	47		36		31	
Service	9		13		14	
Farming, for-						
estry, fishing	0		1		3	
Precision pro-						
duction, draft						
and repair	11		11		13	
Operators,						
laborers	8		9		11	
Armed services	3		0		0	
Total	100	(107)	101	(77,754)§	101	(164,874)§
Income:						
Less than						
$15,000	13		25		29	
$15,000–						
$29,999	34		30		29	
$30,000–						
$49,999	34		28		26	
$50,000 or						
over	19		18		16	
Total	100	(120)	101	(60,826)‖	100	(132,369)‖

Table A.I, cont.

	Sample		U.S. Census* Anchorage		Alaska	
Characteristic	Percent	Number	Percent	Number	Percent	Number
Mean	$32,961		$32,079		$29,797	
Median	$30,000		$27,375		$25,421	
Age at Time of Move:#			N/A		N/A	
16–24	41					
25–29	23					
30 or over	36					
Total	100	(103)				
Mean	28					
Median	26					
Length of Residence in Alaska:						
Less than 5 years	28		N/A		N/A	
5 to 9 years	20					
10 to 19 years	25					
20 years or more	27					
Total	100	(134)				
Mean	12.7 years					
Median	10.5 years					

*Source: U.S. Bureau of The Census, *Census of Population: Detailed Population Characteristics,* 1980.

†Percentages based on number of persons 15 years old and over.

‡Percentages based on number of persons 25 years old and over.

§Percentages based on number of employed civilians 16 years old and over.

‖1979 household income; percentages based on number of households.

#Does not include respondents who were born in Alaska or who moved to Alaska with a parent or guardian.

**N/A = information not available.

Table A.2. Results of Attempts to Interview Respondents Selected for the Anchorage Community Survey, 1979

Result	Percent	
Interview completed	72.8	
Refusal	14.7	
Not home after five attempts	9.2	
Unable to locate dwelling unit	3.3	
Total	100.0	(184)
Dwelling unit unoccupied*		(13)
Dwelling unit non-existent		(3)

*A total of 200 dwelling units was selected, but because 16 of these were either unoccupied or non-existent, the response/non-response rates are based on the 184 units that housed potential respondents.

APPENDIX II

Anchorage Community Survey
Interview Schedule

1. How long have you lived in Alaska?

    1a. Is that all of your life?

    YES   NO

2. While in Alaska, have you always lived in Anchorage?

    YES   NO

    2a. If not, what other place(s) in Alaska did you live? How long did you live there?

IF LIFETIME RESIDENT, SKIP TO QUESTION 18.

3. Where did you live before coming to Alaska? For how long? (Begin with last residence and continue through complete residence history.)

4. Were you employed while living in _____? (Insert name of each previous residence.)

    YES   NO

    4a. If so, what was your occupation there? For how long? (Continue through complete employment history.)

5. Before you moved to Alaska, did you consider moving to some other place(s)?

    YES   NO

5a. If so, where?

5b. Why did you choose Alaska rather than this (these) other place(s)?

6. Did you think life in Alaska would be different from that where you lived before?

YES   NO

6a. If so, in what ways did you think it would be different?

6b. How do you think you got these ideas/notions about Alaska?

6c. Thinking back on it now, do you think that these ideas you had about Alaska before you came were accurate?

Extremely accurate
Somewhat accurate
Don't remember
Not really accurate
Not at all accurate

7. How did your friends react when you told them you were moving to Alaska?

8. How did your family react when you told them you had decided to move?

9. At the time you decided to move to Alaska, did you view the move as permanent or temporary?

Definitely permanent
Probably permanent
Not certain
Probably temporary
Definitely temporary

10. Before you moved, did you know anyone who had visited Alaska?

               YES   NO

    10a. If so, about how many people?

    10b. What was their relation to you (e.g., friend, relative)?

    10c. Where did they visit while in Alaska?

    10d. What did they tell you about their visit?

11. Before you moved, did you know anyone who was already living in Alaska?

               YES   NO

    11a. If so, about how many people?

    11b. What was their relation to you?

    11c. Where were they living?

    11d. What had they told you about living in Alaska?

12. There are probably several reasons why people move to Alaska. From the following list, please tell me whether the reason was EXTREMELY important, VERY important, MODERATELY important, NOT VERY important, or NOT AT ALL important in making your decision to move to Alaska.

    12a. A chance to be independent, to start something new

    12b. Being close to a wilderness environment

    12c. Curiosity about Alaska

    12d. A challenge, an exciting job

    12e. Long-term economic opportunity

12f. To get away from urban problems

12g. To be with family and friends

12h. Immediate income gains

12i. To live a pioneer's life, to be self-reliant

12j. To go to school, to be in the military

12k. Other _____

13. Do you feel that your decision to move to Alaska was:
Entirely a matter of personal choice
Mostly a matter of personal choice
A combination of personal choice and
other circumstances
Mostly due to other circumstances
Entirely due to other circumstances

14. How difficult was the move for you?
Entremely difficult
Very difficult
Moderately difficult
Not very difficult
Not at all difficult

14a. If difficult, in what way(s) was it difficult
(e.g., economic hardship, felt uncomfortable
in a new place)?

15. Did others come with you when you moved to Alaska?
YES   NO

15a. If so, who moved with you (e.g., family,
friends)?

15b. How many others came with you?

16. (If YES to QUESTION 15) How difficult was the move for
those who came with you?

Extremely difficult
Very difficult
Moderately difficult
Not very difficult
Not at all difficult

16a. If difficult, in what way(s) was it difficult for them?

17. Do you consider yourself to be "an Alaskan"?

YES   NO

17a. If so, when did you begin to feel like an Alaskan?

17b. What made you feel that way?

Now I'd like to ask you some questions about life in Alaska in general and more specifically about some of your likes and dislikes about living here. To begin with,

18. What do you like most about living in Alaska? Why?

19. What do you dislike most about living in Alaska? Why?

20. What do you do when you're not at your main job (e.g., other jobs, recreational activities)?

21. When you're not working, how much time do you spend outdoors?

All of it
Most of it
About half of it
Some of it
None of it

22. Have you travelled to other places in Alaska?

YES   NO

22a. If so, where did you go? How did you get there? What was the purpose of your travel (e.g., business or pleasure)?

22b. How did these places compare with Anchorage?

23. Of your closest friends, what proportion live in Alaska?

24. In general, how often do you keep in touch with your closest friends or relatives who live outside of Alaska?

Extremely often
Very often
Somewhat often
Not very often
Not at all often

24a. How often do you write to them?

Extremely often
Very often
Somewhat often
Not very often
Not at all often

24b. How often do you telephone them?

Extremely often
Very often
Somewhat often
Not very often
Not at all often

25. How would you describe most of the people you have met since coming to Alaska?

26. Do you read any newspapers?

YES   NO

26a. If so, which ones?

26b. How often do you read them?

27. Do you read any magazines?

        YES   NO

    27a. If so, which ones?

    28b. How often do you read them?

28. Now I'd like you to describe the BEST DAY you have had in Alaska so far. What made it so special?

29. What about your WORST day? What made is so bad?

IF LIFETIME RESIDENT, SKIP TO QUESTION 32.

30. Do you do things now that you didn't do before you moved to Alaska? For example, some people never skied or hunted before they came to Alaska; others never got involved in local politics or state government.

        YES   NO

    30a. If so, in what activities have you participated?

31. Is the reverse true? That is, are there things you don't do now that you did before you moved to Alaska?

        YES   NO

    31a. If so, what activities?

32. How long do you plan to stay in Alaska?

33. Just as there are several reasons why people come to Alaska, people probably differ as to why they stay once they have moved here. Of the following factors, how would you rate each as a reason for staying in Alaska? Is it EXTREMELY important, VERY important, MODERATELY important, NOT VERY important, or NOT AT ALL important?

    33a. Immediate income gains

33b. A chance to be independent, to start something new

33c. To get away from urban problems

33d. Long-term economic opportunity

33e. Being close to a wilderness environment

33f. A challenge, an exciting job

33g. Curiosity about Alaska

33h. To be with family and friends

33i. To live a pioneer's life, to be self-reliant

33j. To be in school, the military

33k. Consider Anchorage home

33l. No place or job to move to

33m. Don't want to leave job or school

33n. Not enough money to leave

33o. Other _____

34. Since you have lived here, have you known anyone who has moved away from Alaska?

YES   NO

34a. What was their relation to you?

34b. Why do you think they moved?

35. How much of your own food would you say you and your family grow, hunt, fish, or gather for yourselves?

All of it
Most of it
About half of it
Some of it
None of it

36. Which of these activities have you or your family done during the time you have lived in Anchorage?

    36a. Build or help build your own home

    36b. Cut and gather your own firewood

    36c. Sew many of your own clothes

    36d. Repair your own automobile, television, or other appliances

    36e. Use something other than a car, bus, bicycle, or motorcycle to get to work

37. Now I'd like to read you a series of statements that have been used to describe people living in Alaska. I would like to know whether you agree or disagree with these descriptions, as well as whether you think others might agree or disagree with them. Given this set of responses (STRONGLY agree, SOMEWHAT agree, NO OPINION/DON'T KNOW, SOMEWHAT disagree, STRONGLY disagree), please select the one that best characterizes your feelings about the statement.

To begin, how do you feel about the first statement?

    37a. Alaskans are individuals with a great deal of resourcefulness.

        Respondent _____

        How do you think others living in Alaska would respond to this statement?

        Other Alaskans _____

        How do you think those living outside of Alaska would respond to this statement?

        Outsiders _____

        Finally, do you agree or disagree with this statement as it applies to most Americans living outside of Alaska? That is, are *most Americans* individuals with a great deal of resourcefulness?

Description of Outsiders _____

(Repeat line of questioning for remaining statements.)

37b. Alaskans are geographically mobile; they don't stay in one place for long.

37c. Alaskans do a lot of hunting and fishing.

37d. Alaskans are more concerned with making money than with job satisfaction.

37e. Alaskans welcome adventure; they are willing to take a chance.

37f. The natural surroundings of their environment are important to Alaskans.

37g. People in Alaska don't know very much about world affairs.

37h. When it comes to making value judgments, Alaskans rely more on their personal convictions than on the opinions of others.

37i. Alaskans have little respect for tradition; they prefer the old to the new.

37j. When it comes down to it, most Alaskans dislike government intervention.

38. Sex

39. Race

40. Age

41. Marital status

42. Education

    42a. How many years of school have you
         completed?

    42b. What is the highest degree you hold?
         M.D., Ph.D., J.D.
         M.A./M.S.
         B.A./B.S.
         Two- or three-year technical degree
         High school diploma
         Some high school or less

43. Income: Into which of the following categories did your
gross income from last year fall?

Under $3,000	$25,000–29,999
$3,000–4,999	$30,000–39,999
$5,000–7,999	$40,000–49,999
$8,000–11,999	$50,000–59,999
$12,000–14,999	$60,000–69,999
$15,000–19,999	$70,000 or more
$20,000–24,999	No answer

44. Are you currently employed?

               YES   NO

    44a. If so, what is your occupation?

REFERENCES

Alaska Criminal Justice Planning Agency. *Crime in Alaska—1978.* Juneau, AK.: Alaska Criminal Justice Planning Agency, 1979.

Alaska Department of Labor. *Alaska Economic Trends.* Vol. 4, issue 8. Juneau, AK.: Alaska Department of Labor, 1984.

———. *Alaska Population Overview.* Juneau, AK.: Alaska Department of Labor, September, 1985.

Alaska Statehood Commission. *More Perfect Union: A Plan for Action—Final Report by the Alaska Statehood Commission.* Juneau, AK.: Alaska Statehood Commission, January 24, 1983.

———. *More Perfect Union: A Preliminary Report of the Alaska Statehood Commission.* Juneau, AK.: Alaska Statehood Commission, January 19, 1982.

Alaska Transportation Consultants and Dupere and Associates. *International Airport Study for Anchorage and Fairbanks.* Anchorage, AK.: Alaska Transportation Consultants and Dupere and Associates, December, 1980.

Alexander, Fred. *Moving Frontiers: An American Theme and Its Application to Australian History.* Melbourne: Melbourne University Press, 1947.

Anchorage Convention and Visitors Bureau. *1982 Anchorage Visitors Survey.* Anchorage, AK.: Anchorage Convention and Visitors Bureau, March, 1983.

Anchorage Resource Information Service. *Anchorage Quarterly: A Review of Socio-Economic Data.* Vol. 1, no. 1. Anchorage, AK.: Anchorage Resource Information Service, September 30, 1978.

———. *Anchorage Quarterly: A Review of Socio-Economic Data.* Vol. 1, no. 2. Anchorage, AK.: Anchorage Resource Information Service, December 30, 1978.

Arrington, Leonard J., and Davis Bitton. *The Mormon Experience: A History of the Latter-Day Saints.* New York: Alfred A. Knopf, 1979.

Atwood, Evangeline. *Anchorage: All American City.* Portland, OR.: Binfords and Mort, 1957.

Audit Bureau of Circulations. *Magazine Publisher's Statement, Average Paid Circulation for Six Months Ending December 31, 1985, for Alaska Magazine.* Chicago: Audit Bureau of Circulations, 1986.

Baird, Robert. "View of the Valley of the Mississippi, or the Emigrant's and Traveller's Guide to the West, 1834." In *America's Frontier Story: A Documentary History of Westward Expansion.* Edited by Martin Ridge and Ray Allen Billington. New York: Holt, Rinehart and Winston, 1969, pp. 9–11.

Bardo, John W., and Deborah J. Bardo. "From Settlers to Migrants: A Symbolic Interactionist Interpretation of American Migration to Australia." In *Studies in Symbolic Interaction.* Edited by Norman K. Denzin. Greenwich, CT.: JAI Press, 1980, pp. 193–232.

Beirne, Virginia. Interview with author. Anchorage, AK. September, 1979.

Benson, Lee. "The Historian as Mythmaker: Turner and the Closed Frontier." In *The Frontier in American Development: Essays in Honor of Paul Wallace Gates.* Edited by David M. Ellis. Ithaca, N.Y.: Cornell University Press, 1969, pp. 3–19.

Berardo, Felix M. "Kinship Interaction and Communications Among Space-Age Migrants." *Journal of Marriage and the Family* 29 (August, 1967):541–554.

Berger, Peter, and Thomas Luckmann. *The Social Construction of Reality.* New York: Doubleday, 1967.

Biddle, Bruce J., et al. "Shared Inaccuracies in the Role of the Teacher." In *Role Theory: Concepts and Research.* Edited by Bruce J. Biddle and Edwin J. Thomas. New York: John Wiley and Sons, 1966, pp. 302–310.

Bieder, Robert E. "Kinship as a Factor in Migration." *Journal of Marriage and the Family* 35 (August, 1973):429–439.

Billington, Ray Allen. *The American Frontier.* Washington, D.C.: American Historical Association, 1958.

———. *America's Frontier Heritage.* Albuquerque, N.M.: University of New Mexico Press, 1974.

Boatright, Mody C. "The Myth of Frontier Individualism." *Southwestern Social Science Quarterly* 22 (June, 1941):14–32.

Bogue, Allan G. "Social Theory and the Pioneer." In *Turner and the Sociology of the Frontier.* Edited by Richard Hofstadter and Seymour Martin Lipset. New York: Basic Books, 1968, pp. 73–99.

Bogue, Donald J. "A Migrant's-Eye View of the Costs and Benefits of Migration to a Metropolis." In *Internal Migration: A Comparative Perspective.* Edited by Alan A. Brown and Egon Neuberger. New York: Academic Press, 1977, pp. 167–182.

———. *Principles of Demography.* New York: John Wiley and Sons, 1969.

Boorstin, Donald J. *The Image: A Guide to Pseudo-Events in America.* New York: Harper and Row, 1961.

Bourne, L. S., and M. I. Logan. "Changing Urbanization Patterns at the Margin: The Examples of Australia and Canada." In *Urbanization and Counter-Urbanization.* Edited by Brian J. L. Berry. Beverly Hills, CA.: Sage, 1976, pp. 111–143.

Brewer, Marilynn B., and Donald T. Campbell. *Ethnocentrism and Intergroup Attitudes: East African Evidence.* New York: John Wiley and Sons, 1976.

Brown, James S., Harry K. Schwarzweller, and Joseph J. Mangalam. "Kentucky Mountain Migration and the Stem-Family: An American Variation on a Theme by LePlay." *Rural Sociology* 28 (March, 1963):48–69.

Browning, Harley L., and Waltraut Feindt. "Selectivity of

Migrants to a Metropolis in a Developing Country: A Mexican Case Study." *Demography* 6 (November, 1969):347–357.

Bryce, James. "The American Commonwealth." In *The West: Contemporary Records of America's Expansion Across the Continent: 1607–1890.* Edited by Bayrd Still. New York: Capricorn Books, 1961, pp. 265–267.

Byrns, Richard. "Literary Fog over Alaska." *Trace* 42 (Summer, 1961):158–163.

Choldin, Harvey M. "Kinship Networks in the Migration Process." *International Migration Review* 7 (Summer, 1973):163–175.

Clark, George N. *The Seventeenth Century.* Oxford: Oxford University Press, 1947.

Clark, John A. "Oddities of a Pioneer Town—Including Dogs, Cats and Chickens." In *Sourdough Sagas.* Edited by Herbert L. Heller. Cleveland, OH.: World Publishing Company, 1967, pp. 247–257.

Cohen, Cassey M. "How to Walk, Talk and Eat like a Texan." *Texas Woman* (August, 1979):40–44.

Courchene, Thomas J. "Interprovincial Migration and Economic Adjustment." *Canadian Journal of Economics* 3 (November, 1970):550–576.

Crevecoeur, J. Hector St. John de. *Letters from an American Farmer.* New York: E. P. Dutton and Company, 1957.

De Amicis, John. "It Just Happened: The Transformation of American Migrants in Australia from Sojourners to Settlers." *Australian and New Zealand Journal of Sociology* 12 (June, 1976):136–144.

Dittman Research Corporation. *National Alaska Attitude Survey.* Anchorage, AK.: Dittman Research Corporation, April 17, 1981.

Dwight, Timothy. *Travels; in New England and New-York, Volume 2.* New Haven, CT.: Timothy Dwight, 1821–1822.

Effrat, Marcia Pelly. "Approaches to Community: Conflicts

and Complementaries." In *The Community: Approaches and Applications*. Edited by Marcia Pelly Effrat. New York: Free Press, 1974, pp. 1–32.

Elkins, Stanley, and Eric McKitrick. "A Meaning for Turner's Frontier: Democracy in the Old Northwest." *Political Science Quarterly* 69 (September, 1954):321–353.

Ender, Richard L. *1978 Population Profile: Municipality of Anchorage*. Anchorage, AK.: Municipality of Anchorage, 1979.

Fischer, Claude S. "Toward a Subcultural Theory of Urbanism." *American Journal of Sociology* 80 (May, 1975):1,319–1,341.

Gans, Herbert J. *The Urban Villagers*. New York: Free Press, 1962.

Gardey, Jon. *Alaska: The Sophisticated Wilderness*. New York: Stein and Day, 1976.

Giddings, Franklin H. *Studies in the Theory of Human Society*. New York: Macmillan, 1922.

Godkin, Edwin L. "Aristocratic Opinions of Democracy." In *American's Frontier Story*. Edited by Martin Ridge and Ray Allen Billington. New York: Holt, Rinehart and Winston, 1969, pp. 13–16.

Goffman, Erving. *Asylums*. Garden City, N.Y.: Anchor, 1961.

Goldman, Robert, and David R. Dickens. "The Selling of Rural America." *Rural Sociology* 48 (Winter, 1983):585–606.

Goldstein, Sidney. "The Extent of Repeated Migration: An Analysis Based on the Danish Population Register." *Journal of the American Statistical Association* 59 (December, 1964):1,121–1,132.

Gouldner, Alvin. "Reciprocity and Autonomy in Functional Theory." In *Symposium on Sociological Theory*. Edited by Llewellyn Gross. Evanston, IL.: Peterson and Company, 1959, pp. 241–270.

Graburn, Nelson H. H. "Tourism: The Sacred Journey." In

Hosts and Guests: The Anthropology of Tourism.
Edited by Valene L. Smith. Philadelphia: University of
Pennsylvania Press, 1977, pp. 17-31.

Gruening, Ernest. *The State of Alaska.* New York: Random
House, 1954.

Gusfield, Joseph R. *Community.* New York: Harper and
Row, 1975.

Hamilton, C. Horace. "The Negro Leaves the South." *Demography* 1, no. 1 (1964):273-295.

Hammond, Jay. Interview with Larry Makinson. Juneau,
AK. June, 1979.

Hanrahan, John, and Peter Gruenstein. *Lost Frontier: The
Marketing of Alaska.* New York: W. W. Norton and
Company, 1977.

Hayes, Carlton J. H. "The American Frontier—Frontier of
What?" *American Historical Review* 51 (January,
1946):199-216.

Herring, Douglas. "Alaska: Synopsis of the Show Including
the Lyrics," mimeograph, 1978.

Hillary, George A., Jr. "Definitions of Community: Areas of
Agreement." *Rural Sociology* 20 (June, 1955):111-123.

Hunt, William R. *Alaska: A Bicentennial History.* New
York: W. W. Norton and Company, 1976.

Hunter, Albert. *Symbolic Communities.* Chicago: University
of Chicago Press, 1974.

Jacobs, Jane. *The Death and Life of Great American Cities.*
New York: Random House, 1961.

Jansen, Clifford J. "Migration: A Sociological Problem." In
Readings in the Sociology of Migration. Edited by
Clifford J. Jansen. New York: Pergamon Press, 1970,
pp. 3-35.

Jody, Marilyn. "Alaska in the American Literary Imagination: A Literary History of Frontier Alaska with a
Bibliographical Guide to the Study of Alaskan Literature." Ph.D. thesis, Indiana University, 1969.

Juricek, John T. "American Usage of the Word 'Frontier'
from Colonial Times to Frederick Jackson Turner."

Proceedings of the American Philosophical Society 110 (February, 1960):10–34.

Kane, Murray. "Some Considerations of the Safety Valve Doctrine." *Mississippi Valley Historical Review* 23 (September, 1936):169–188.

Kanter, Rosabeth Moss. *Commitment and Community.* Cambridge, MA.: Harvard University Press, 1972.

Kerchoff, Alan C., and Thomas C. McCormick. "Marginal Status and Marginal Personality." *Social Forces* 32 (October, 1955):48–55.

Khazanov, A. M. *Nomads and the Outside World.* Translated by Julia Crookenden. New York: Cambridge University Press, 1984.

Kresge, David T., Thomas A. Morehouse, and George W. Rogers. *Issues in Alaska Development.* Seattle: University of Washington Press, 1977.

Land, Kenneth C. "Duration of Residence and Prospective Migration: Further Evidence." *Demography* 6 (May, 1969):133–140.

Lansing, John B., and Eva Mueller. *The Geographic Mobility of Labor.* Ann Arbor, MI.: University of Michigan Press, 1967.

Lee, Everett S. "The Turner Thesis Re-examined." *American Quarterly* 8 (Spring, 1961):77–83.

Lengyel, Peter. "A Rejoinder." *International Social Science Journal* 27, no. 4 (1975):753–757.

Lerner, Max. *America as a Civilization.* New York: Simon and Schuster, 1957.

LeVine, Robert A., and Donald T. Campbell. *Ethnocentrism: Theories of Conflict, Ethnic Attitudes, and Group Behavior.* New York: John Wiley and Sons, 1972.

Leyburn, James G. *Frontier Folkways.* New Haven, CT.: Yale University Press, 1935.

Liebow, Elliot. *Tally's Corner.* Boston: Little, Brown, 1967.

Litwak, Eugene. "Geographic Mobility and Extended Family Cohesion." *American Sociological Review* 25 (June, 1960):385–394.

Long, Larry H. "Migration Differentials by Education and Occupation: Trends and Variations." *Demography* 10 (May, 1973):243–258.

———, and K. A. Hansen. "Reasons for Interstate Migration: Jobs, Retirement, Climate, and Other Influences." *Current Population Reports.* Series P23, no. 81. Washington, D.C.: U.S. Department of Commerce, Bureau of the Census, 1979.

Loomis, Charles. *Social Relationships and Institutions in Seven New Rural Communities.* Washington, D.C.: Government Printing Office, 1940.

McInnis, Marvin. "Age, Education and Occupation Differentials in Interregional Migration: Some Evidence for Canada." *Demography* 8 (May, 1971):195–203.

McLemore, S. Dale. "Simmel's Stranger: A Critique of the Concept." *Pacific Sociological Review* 13 (Spring, 1970):86–94.

McPhee, John. *Coming into the Country.* New York: Farrar, Straus and Giroux, 1977.

Maines, David R. "Bodies and Selves: Notes on a Fundamental Dilemma in Demography." In *Studies in Symbolic Interaction.* Edited by Norman K. Denzin. Greenwich, CT.: JAI Press, 1978, pp. 241–265.

Malin, James C. "Space and History: Reflections on the Closed-Space Doctrines of Turner and Mackinder." *Agricultural History* 18 (1944):65–74, 107–126.

Melbin, Murray. "Night as Frontier." *American Sociological Review* 43 (February, 1978):3–22.

Miller, Ann R. "Interstate Migrants in the United States: Some Socio-Economic Differences by Type of Move." *Demography* 14 (February, 1977):1–17.

Mills, C. Wright. "Language, Logic and Culture." *American Sociological Review* 4 (October, 1939):670–680.

Mood, Fulmer. "Notes on the History of the Word Frontier." *Agricultural History* 22 (April, 1948):78–83.

Morrison, Peter A. "Chronic Movers and the Future Redistribution of Population: A Longitudinal Analysis." *Demography* 8 (May, 1971):171–184.

————. "Duration of Residence and Prospective Migration: The Evaluation of a Stochastic Model." *Demography* 4 (1967):553–561.

————, and Judith P. Wheeler. "The Image of 'Elsewhere' in the American Tradition of Migration." In *Human Migration: Patterns and Policies.* Edited by William H. McNeill and Ruth S. Adams. Bloomington, IN.: Indiana University Press, 1978, pp. 75–84.

Municipality of Anchorage. Department of Health and Environmental Protection. *1979 Annual Report.* Anchorage, AK.: Municipality of Anchorage, 1980.

Nash, Roderick, *Wilderness and the American Mind.* New Haven, CT.: Yale University Press, 1973.

Nixon, Herman Clarence. "Precursors of Turner in the Interpretation of the American Frontier." *South Atlantic Quarterly* 28 (January, 1929):83–89.

Park, Robert E. "Human Migration and the Marginal Man." *American Journal of Sociology* 33 (May, 1928):881–893.

Pierson, George Wilson. "The Frontier and American Institutions: A Criticism of the Turner Theory." *New England Quarterly* 16 (June, 1942):224–255.

————. "The Frontier and Frontiersmen of Turner's Essays: A Scrutiny of the Foundations of the Middle Western Tradition." *Pennsylvania Magazine of History and Biography* 64 (October, 1940):449–478.

————. *The Moving American.* New York: Alfred A. Knopf, 1973.

Pomeroy, Earl. "The Significance of Continuity." In *The Frontier Thesis: Valid Interpretation of American History?* Edited by Ray Allen Billington. New York: Holt, Rinehart and Winston, 1966, pp. 80–89.

Price, Donald O. "Rural to Urban Migration of Mexican-Americans, Negroes, and Anglos." *International Migration Review* 5 (Fall, 1971):281–291.

Ravenstein, E. G. "The Laws of Migration." *Journal of the Royal Statistical Society* 48 (June, 1885):167–227.

Research Design Productions. *The Anchorage Factbook—1983.* Anchorage, AK.: Research Design Productions, 1983.

Riegel, Robert E. *America Moves West*. New York: H. Holt and Company, 1956.

Riesman, David. Individualism Reconsidered and Other Essays. Glencoe, IL.: Free Press, 1954.

Ritchey, P. Neal. "Explanations of Migration." In *Annual Review of Sociology*. Edited by Alex Inkeles. Palo Alto, CA.: Annual Reviews, 1976, pp. 363–404.

Rogers, George W. "Economic Effects of the Earthquake." In *The Great Alaska Earthquake of 1964: Human Ecology*. Edited by the National Research Council. Washington, D.C.: Government Printing Office, 1970a, pp. 58–76.

———. "Impact of the Earthquake on the Economy of Alaska." In *The Great Alaska Earthquake of 1964: Human Ecology*. Edited by the National Research Council. Washington, D.C.: Government Printing Office, 1970b, pp. 32–38.

———. "Wilderness and Development in Alaska." In *Alaska Public Policy: Current Problems and Issues*. Edited by G. S. Harrison. College, AK.: Institute for Social, Economic and Government Research, 1973, pp. 229–238.

Rogers, Tommy W. "Prior Moves as a Migration Differential Factor." *Rocky Mountain Social Science Journal* 5 (October, 1968):119–126.

Rose, A. M. "Distance of Migration and Socio-Economic Status of Migrants." In *Readings in the Sociology of Migration*. Edited by Clifford J. Jansen. New York: Pergamon Press, 1970, pp. 85–92.

Schafer, Joseph. "Was the West a Safety Valve for Labor?" *Mississippi Valley Historical Review* 24 (December, 1937):299–314.

Shannon, Fred A. "A Post-Mortem on the Labor-Safety-Valve Theory." *Agricultural History* 19 (January, 1945):31–37.

Sharp, Paul F. "Three Frontiers: Some Comparative Studies of Canadian, American and Australian Settlement." *Pacific Historical Review* 24 (November, 1955): 369–377.

Shaw, R. Paul. *Migration Theory and Fact.* Philadelphia: Regional Science Research Institute, 1975.

Shibutani, Tomatsu. *Society and Personality.* Englewood Cliffs, N.J.: Prentice-Hall, 1961.

———, and Kian M. Kwan. *Ethnic Stratification.* Toronto: Macmillan, 1965.

Shils, Edward. *Center and Periphery: Essays in Macrosociology.* Chicago: University of Chicago Press, 1975.

Shryrock, Henry S. *Population Mobility Within the United States.* Chicago: University of Chicago Press, 1964.

Simmel, Georg. "The Stranger." In *The Sociology of George Simmel.* Edited by Kurt H. Wolff. New York: Free Press, 1950.

Smiler, Norman J. "The Safety-Valve Doctrine Reevaluated." *Agricultural History* 32 (October, 1958):250–257.

Smith, Henry Nash. *Virgin Land: The American West as Symbol and Myth.* New York: Vintage Books, 1950.

Smith, Lynn. "Sourdough Life." In *Sourdough Sagas.* Edited by Herbert L. Heller, Cleveland, OH.: World Publishing Company, 1967, pp. 125–168.

Smith, Valene L., editor. *Hosts and Guests: The Anthropology of Tourism.* Philadelphia: University of Pennsylvania Press, 1977.

Stouffer, Samuel A. "Intervening Opportunities and Competing Migrants." *Journal of Regional Science* 2 (Spring, 1960):1–26.

———. "Intervening Opportunities: A Theory Relating Mobility and Distance." *American Sociological Review* 5 (December, 1940):845–867.

Strauss, Anselm. *Images of the American City.* New Brunswick, N.J.: Transaction Books, 1976.

———. *Mirrors and Masks.* Glencoe, IL.: Free Press, 1959.

Taeuber, Karl E., Leonard Chiazze, Jr., and William Haenszel. *Migration in the United States: An Analysis of Residence Histories.* Public Health Monograph No. 77. Washington, D.C.: Government Printing Office, 1968.

Thernstrom, Stephen, and Peter R. Knights. "Men in Motion: Some Data and Speculations About Urban Population Mobility in Nineteenth-Century America." *Journal of Inter-Disciplinary History* 1 (Autumn, 1970):7–35.

Thomas, Dorothy S. "Age and Economic Differentials in Interstate Migration." *Population Index* 24 (October, 1958):313–325.

Tilly, Charles, and C. H. Brown. "On Uprooting, Kinship and the Auspices of Migration." *International Journal of Comparative Sociology* 8 (1968):139–164.

Tocqueville, Alexis de. *Democracy in America.* Edited by Richard D. Heffner. New York: New American Library, 1956.

Toney, Michael B. "The Simultaneous Examination of Economic and Social Factors in Destination Selection: Employing Objective and Subjective Measures." *Demography* 15 (May, 1978):205–212.

Triandis, Harry C. *The Analysis of Subjective Culture.* New York: John Wiley and Sons, 1972.

Turner, Frederick Jackson. *The Frontier in American History.* New York: H. Holt and Company, 1920.

Uhlenberg, Peter. "Noneconomic Determinants of Non-migration: Sociological Considerations for Migration Theory." *Rural Sociology* 38 (Fall, 1973):296–311.

U.S. Department of Commerce, Bureau of the Census. *Census of Business: Retail Trade, Area Statistics,* 1948, 1954, 1958, 1963, 1967.

———. *Census of Business: Service Industries, Area Statistics,* 1948, 1954, 1958, 1963, 1967.

———. *Census of Business: Wholesale Trade, Area Statistics,* 1948, 1954, 1958, 1963, 1967.

———. *Census of Retail Trade: Area Statistics,* 1972, 1977, 1982.

———. *Census of Population,* 1920, 1929, 1939, 1950, 1960, 1970, 1980.

———. *Census of Service Industries: Area Statistics,* 1972, 1977, 1982.

———. *Census of Wholesale Trade: Area Statistics,* 1972, 1977, 1982.

———. *Geographic Mobility: March 1975 to March 1978. Current Population Reports.* Series P-20, no. 331, 1978.

———. *Estimates of the Population of Counties and Metropolitan Areas: July 1, 1977 and 1978,* 1978.

———. *State of Residence in 1975 by State of Residence in 1980,* PC80-S1-9, March, 1983.

U.S. Department of Labor, Bureau of Labor Statistics. *Employment and Earnings, States and Areas, 1977-81,* 1982.

Vogt, Evon. *Modern Homesteaders: The Life of a Twentieth Century Frontier Community.* Cambridge, MA.: Harvard University Press, 1955.

Wadycki, Walter J. "Alternative Opportunities and Interstate Migration: Some Additional Results." *Review of Economics and Statistics* 56 (May, 1974):254-257.

Wallerstein, Immanuel. *The Modern World System: Capitalist Agriculture and the Origins of the European World-Economy in the Sixteenth Century.* New York: Academic Press, 1974.

———. *The Modern World System II: Mercantilism and the Consolidation of the European World Economy, 1600-1750.* New York: Academic Press, 1980.

Watson, J. Wreford. "Image Geography: The Myth of America in the American Scene." *Advancement of Science* 27 (September, 1970):71-79.

Webber, Melvin. "Order in Diversity: Community Without Propinquity." In *Cities and Space: The Future Use of Urban Land.* Edited by L. Wingo. Baltimore: Johns Hopkins University Press, 1963.

Weber, Adna Ferrin. *The Growth of Cities in the Nineteenth Century: A Study in Statistics.* Ithaca, N.Y.: Cornell University Press, 1967.

Weeden, Robert B. "Man in Nature: A Strategy for Alaskan Living." In *Alaska Public Policy: Current Problems and Issues.* Edited by G. S. Harrison. College, AK.: Institute for Social, Economic, and Government Research, 1973.

Wellman, Barry. "The Community Question: The Intimate Networks of East Yorkers." *American Journal of Sociology* 84 (March, 1979):1,201-1,231.

Welter, Rush. "The Frontier West as Image of American Society: 1776–1860." *Pacific Northwest Quarterly* 52 (January, 1961):1–6.

White, Morton, and Lucia White. *The Intellectual Versus the City: From Thomas Jefferson to Frank Lloyd Wright.* New York: Oxford University Press, 1977.

Whyte, William F. *Street Corner Society.* Chicago: University of Chicago Press, 1943.

Willits, Fern K., and Robert C. Bealer, and Donald M. Crider. "Migrant Status and Success: A Panel Study." *Rural Sociology* 43 (Fall, 1978):386–402.

Winks, Robin. *The Myth of the American Frontier: Its Relevance to America, Canada and Australia.* Leicester, U.K.: Leicester University Press, 1971.

Ziff-Davis Publishing Company. *Travel Market Yearbook.* Cherry Hill, N.J.: Ziff-Davis Publishing Company, 1980.

INDEX